Lecture Notes in Artificial  573

Subseries of Lecture Notes in Computer Science

LNAI Series Editors

Randy Goebel
University of Alberta, Edmonton, Canada
Yuzuru Tanaka
Hokkaido University, Sapporo, Japan
Wolfgang Wahlster
DFKI and Saarland University, Saarbrücken, Germany

LNAI Founding Series Editor

Joerg Siekmann
DFKI and Saarland University, Saarbrücken, Germany

Domenico Beneventano   Zoran Despotovic
Francesco Guerra   Sam Joseph   Gianluca Moro
Adrián Perreau de Pinninck (Eds.)

Agents and Peer-to-Peer Computing

7th International Workshop, AP2PC 2008
Estoril, Portugal, May 13, 2008 and
8th International Workshop, AP2PC 2009
Budapest, Hungary, May 11, 2009
Revised Selected Papers

 Springer

Series Editors

Randy Goebel, University of Alberta, Edmonton, Canada
Jörg Siekmann, University of Saarland, Saarbrücken, Germany
Wolfgang Wahlster, DFKI and University of Saarland, Saarbrücken, Germany

Volume Editors

Domenico Beneventano
Francesco Guerra
Università di Modena e Reggio Emilia, via Vignolese 905, 41100 Modena, Italy
E-mail: {domenico.beneventano; francesco.guerra@unimore.it}

Zoran Despotovic
DOCOMO Euro-Labs, Landsberger Str. 312, 80687 Munich, Germany
E-mail: despotovic@docomolab-euro.com

Sam Joseph
Hawai'i Pacific University, 1164 Bishop Street, Honolulu, HI 96813, USA
E-mail: sjoseph@hpu.edu

Gianluca Moro
Università di Bologna, via Venezia 52, 47521 Cesena, Italy
E-mail: gianluca.moro@unibo.it

Adrián Perreau de Pinninck
CSIC - Spanish National Research Council, 08193 Bellaterra, Spain
E-mail: adrianp@iiia.csic.es

ISSN 0302-9743   e-ISSN 1611-3349
ISBN 978-3-642-31808-5   e-ISBN 978-3-642-31809-2
DOI 10.1007/978-3-642-31809-2
Springer Heidelberg Dordrecht London New York

Library of Congress Control Number: 2012941671

CR Subject Classification (1998): I.2.11, I.2, C.2.4, C.2, H.4, H.3, K.4.4

LNCS Sublibrary: SL 7 – Artificial Intelligence

Typesetting: Camera-ready by author, data conversion by Scientific Publishing Services, Chennai, India

Printed on acid-free paper

Springer is part of Springer Science+Business Media (www.springer.com)

Preface

Peer-to-peer (P2P) computing has been attracting significant attention from both academia and industry researchers. Many studies show that P2P traffic constitutes the largest part of the total Internet traffic, most of which is generated by file distribution (e.g., BitTorrent) and video streaming (e.g., Sopcast, PPLive) P2P applications. This attention is now being transferred to standardization bodies as well, as IETF's Application Layer Traffic Optimization Working Group demonstrates.

Decentralization and self-organization are the key principles of the P2P computing. The entire system operation is highly influenced by choices and decisions of individual peers. Yet, the entire system must operate in a state that is socially desirable, even though there is no central coordination. The success of P2P systems strongly depends on a number of factors. The ability to limit and control "free riding." P2P systems become efficient and useful only if every peer provides its computing resources, as opposed to only consuming resources provided by others. Thus, equitable provisioning of resources is crucial, as are economic models which rely on incentive mechanisms to control and mitigate the free-riding problem. Further, the ability to enforce provision of trusted services is also very important. To this end, reputation-based P2P trust models are recognized by the research community as a viable solution. Their design is challenging as they must be at the same time scalable and provide mechanisms to the interested users that can deter untrusted behavior.

Although researchers working on distributed computing, multiagent systems, databases and networks have been using similar concepts for a long time, it is only fairly recently that papers motivated by the current P2P paradigm have started appearing in high-quality conferences and workshops. Research in agent systems in particular appears to be most relevant because, since their inception, multiagent systems have always been thought of as collections of peers.

The International Workshop on Agents and Peer-to-Peer Computing is co-located with the International Joint Conference on Autonomous Agents and Multi Agent Systems (AAMAS). There are good reasons for this. P2P protocols can work only if they are structured in such a way to bring benefits to the individual peers. This is where the P2P paradigm approaches the multiagent paradigm. The emphasis in this context on decentralization, user autonomy, dynamic growth and other advantages of P2P also leads to significant potential problems. Most prominent among these problems are coordination: the ability of an agent to make decisions on its own actions in the context of activities of other agents; and scalability: the value of the P2P systems lies in how well they scale along several dimensions, including complexity, heterogeneity of peers, robustness, traffic redistribution, and so forth. It is important to scale up coordination strategies along multiple dimensions to enhance their tractability and viability, and thereby to widen potential application domains. These two problems are common to many large-scale applications. Without coordination, agents may be wasting their efforts, squandering resources and failing to achieve their objectives in situations requiring collective effort.

Just like its previous editions, this workshop too brought together researchers working on agent systems and P2P computing with the intention of strengthening this link. Researchers from other related areas such as distributed systems, networks and database systems were also welcome (and, in our opinion, have a lot to contribute). The following is a non-exhaustive list of topics of special interest:

- Intelligent agent techniques for P2P computing
- P2P computing techniques for multiagent systems
- The Semantic Web and semantic coordination mechanisms for P2P systems
- Scalability, coordination, robustness and adaptability in P2P systems
- Self-organization and emergent behavior in P2P systems
- E-commerce and P2P computing
- Social networks, community of interest building, regulation and behavioral norms P2P data-mining agents
- Participation and contract incentive mechanisms in P2P systems
- Computational models of trust and reputation
- Community of interest building and regulation, and behavioral norms
- Intellectual property rights and legal issues in P2P systems
- P2P architectures
- Scalable data structures for P2P systems
- Services in P2P systems (service definition languages, service discovery, filtering and composition etc.)
- Knowledge discovery and P2P data-mining agents
- P2P-oriented information systems
- Mobile P2P
- Information ecosystems and P2P systems
- Security considerations in P2P networks
- Ad-hoc networks and pervasive computing based on P2P architectures and wireless communication devices
- Grid computing solutions based on agents and P2P paradigms
- Legal issues in P2P networks and intellectual property rights in P2P systems

The workshop series emphasizes discussions on methodologies, models, algorithms and technologies, strengthening the connection between agents and P2P computing. These objectives are accomplished by bringing together researchers and contributions from these two disciplines but also from more traditional areas such as distributed systems, networks, and databases.

This volume contains the proceedings of AP2PC 2008 and 2009, the 7th and 8th International Workshop on Agents and Peer-to-Peer Computing [1]. Both

---

[1] http://p2p.ingce.unibo.it/

editions were held in conjunction with the International Joint Conference on Autonomous Agents and Multi Agent Systems (AAMAS), the 2008 edition was in Estoril, Portugal, on May 13, 2008, while the last one was held in Budapest, Hungary (11 May 2009). The volume contains the papers presented at the workshops, fully revised to incorporate reviewers' comments and discussions.

We would like to thank the invited speakers of the seventh and eighth editions, respectively, Katia Sycara, Director of the Intelligent Software Agents Lab at the Carnegie Mellon University, Pittsburgh, USA, Sandip Sen, University of Tulsa, Tulsa, OK, USA, Frances Brazier, Vrije Universiteit Amsterdam, The Netherlands, and Giacomo Cabri, University of Modena and Reggio Emilia, Italy.

After distributing the call for papers for the workshop, we received 16 papers in the seventh edition and 8 in the eighth. All submissions were reviewed for scope and quality, eight were accepted to be published as full papers in the seventh edition, three in the eighth. We would like to thank the authors for their submissions and the members of the Program Committee for reviewing the papers under time pressure and for their support for the workshop. Finally, we would like to acknowledge the Steering Committee for its guidance and encouragement.

These workshops followed the successful sixth edition held in conjunction with AAMAS in Honolulu, Hawaii, in 2007. In recognition of the interdisciplinary nature of P2P computing, a sister event called the International Workshop on Databases, Information Systems, and P2P Computing[2] was held in Auckland, New Zealand, in August 2008 in conjunction with the International Conference on Very Large Data Bases (VLDB).

Domenico Beneventano
Zoran Despotovic
Francesco Guerra
Sam Joseph
Gianluca Moro
Adrián Perreau de Pinninck

---

[2] http://dbisp2p.ingce.unibo.it/

Organization

Executive Committees

Organizers of the Seventh Edition
Program Co-chairs

Adrián Perreau de Pinninck	Artificial Intelligence Research Institute
	Spanish National Research Council, Spain
Domenico Beneventano	University of Modena and Reggio-Emilia, Italy
Gianluca Moro	University of Bologna, Italy
Sam Joseph	Hawai'i Pacific University, USA
Zoran Despotovic	Ubiquitous Networking Research Group
	DOCOMO Euro-Labs, Germany

Invited Panelists

Boi Faltings	EPFL, Lausanne, Switzerland
Maria Gini	University of Minnesota, USA
Katia Sycara	Carnegie Mellon University, USA

Steering Committee

Karl Aberer	EPFL, Lausanne, Switzerland
Sonia Bergamaschi	University of Modena and Reggio-Emilia, Italy
Manolis Koubarakis	National and Kapodistrian University of
	Athens, Greece
Paul Marrow	Intelligent Systems Laboratory, BTexact
	Technologies, UK
Gianluca Moro	University of Bologna, Italy
Aris M. Ouksel	University of Illinois at Chicago, USA
Claudio Sartori	CNR-CSITE, University of Bologna, Italy
Munindar P. Singh	North Carolina State University, USA

Program Committee

Karl Aberer	EPFL, Switzerland
Alessandro Agostini	ITC-IRST Trento, Italy
Makoto Amamiya	Kyushu University, Japan
Djamal Benslimane	Université Claude Bernard, France
Sonia Bergamaschi	University of Modena and Reggio-Emilia, Italy
Costas Courcoubetis	AUEB, Greece
Alfredo Cuzzocrea	University of Calabria, Italy

Zoran Despotovic	DOCOMO Communications Laboratory, Germany
Maria Gini	University of Minnesota, USA
Bradley Goldsmith	University of Tasmania, Australia
Francesco Guerra	University of Modena and Reggio-Emilia, Italy
Sam Joseph	Hawai'i Pacific University, USA
Shinichi Honiden	NII, Tokio, Japan
Birgitta König-Ries	University of Karlsruhe, Germany
Zakaria Maamar	Zayed University, UAE
Alberto Montresor	University of Trento, Italy
Gianluca Moro	University of Bologna, Italy
Elth Ogston	Vrije Universiteit Amsterdam, The Netherlands
Andrea Omicini	University of Bologna, Italy
Thanasis Papaioannou	AUEB, Greece
Adrián Perreau de Pinninck	IIIA-CSIC, Barcelona, Spain
Paolo Petta	Austrian Research Institute for AI, Austria
Dimitris Plexousakis	Institute of Computer Science FORTH, Greece
Martin Purvis	University of Otago, New Zealand
Omer F. Rana	Cardiff University, UK
Douglas S. Reeves	North Carolina State University, USA
Claudio Sartori	University of Bologna, Italy
Heng Tao Shen	University of Queensland, Australia
Kian-Lee Tan	National University of Singapore, Singapore
Francisco Valverde-Albacete	Universidad Carlos III de Madrid, Spain
Maurizio Vincini	University of Modena and Reggio-Emilia, Italy
Fang Wang	British Telecom Group, UK
Steven Willmott	3scale networks, Spain

Organizers of the Eighth Edition

Program Co-Chairs

Gianluca Moro	University of Bologna, Italy
Adrin Perreau de Pinninck	Artificial Intelligence Research Institute (IIIA - CSIC) Spanish National Research Council, Spain
Francesco Guerra	University of Modena and Reggio-Emilia, Italy

Steering Committee

Karl Aberer	EPFL, Lausanne, Switzerland
Sonia Bergamaschi	University of Modena and Reggio-Emilia, Italy
Manolis Koubarakis	National and Kapodistrian University of Athens, Greece
Paul Marrow	Intelligent Systems Laboratory, BTexact Technologies, UK

Gianluca Moro	University of Bologna, Italy
Aris M. Ouksel	University of Illinois at Chicago, USA
Claudio Sartori	IEIIT-BO-CNR, University of Bologna, Italy
Munindar P. Singh	North Carolina State University, USA

Program Committee

Karl Aberer	EPFL, Switzerland
Alessandro Agostini	ITC-IRST Trento, Italy
Makoto Amamiya	Kyushu University, Japan
Djamal Benslimane	Université Claude Bernard, France
Sonia Bergamaschi	University of Modena and Reggio-Emilia, Italy
Alfredo Cuzzocrea	University of Calabria, Italy
Zoran Despotovic	DoCoMo Communications Laboratory, Germany
Maria Gini	University of Minnesota, USA
Bradley Goldsmith	University of Tasmania, Australia
Francesco Guerra	University of Modena and Reggio-Emilia, Italy
Birgitta Knig-Ries	University of Karlsruhe, Germany
Alberto Montresor	University of Trento, Italy
Gianluca Moro	University of Bologna, Italy
Andrea Omicini	University of Bologna, Italy
Thanasis Papaioannou	Athens University of Economics and Business, Greece
Adrian Perreau de Pinninck	IIIA-CSIC, Barcelona, Spain
Paolo Petta	Austrian Research Institute for AI, Austria
Dimitris Plexousakis	Institute of Computer Science, FORTH, Greece
Martin Purvis	University of Otago, New Zealand
Claudio Sartori	University of Bologna, Italy
Boon-Chong Seet	Auckland University of Technology, New Zealand
Nigel Stanger	University of Otago, New Zealand
Heng Tao Shen	University of Queensland, Australia
Maurizio Vincini	University of Modena and Reggio-Emilia, Italy
Fang Wang	British Telecom Group, UK

Preceding Editions of AP2PC

References to the preceding editions of AP2PC, including the volumes of revised and invited papers, are as follows:

- AP2PC 2002 was held in Bologna, Italy, July 15, 2002. The website can be found at http://p2p.ingce.unibo.it/2002/ The proceedings were published by Springer as LNCS volume no. 2530 and are available online here: http://www.springerlink.com/content/978-3-540-40538-2/

- AP2PC 2003 was held in Melbourne, Australia, July 14, 2003. The website can be found at http://p2p.ingce.unibo.it/2003/ The proceedings were published by Springer as LNCS volume no. 2872 and are available online here: http://www.springerlink.com/content/978-3-540-24053-2/
- AP2PC 2004 was held in New York City, USA, July 19, 2004. The website can be found at http://p2p.ingce.unibo.it/2004/ The proceedings were published by Springer as LNCS volume no. 3601 and are available online here: http://www.springerlink.com/content/978-3-540-29755-0/
- AP2PC 2005 was held in Utrecht, The Netherlands, May 9, 2005. The website can be found at http://p2p.ingce.unibo.it/2005/ The proceedings were published by Springer as LNAI volume no. 4118 and are available online here: http://www.springerlink.com/content/978-3-540-49025-8/
- AP2PC 2006 was held in Hakodate, Japan, May 9, 2006. The web site can be found at http://p2p.ingce.unibo.it/2006/ The proceedings were published by Springer as LNCS volume no. 4461 and are available online here: http://www.springerlink.com/content/n0t745r35482/
- AP2PC 2007 was held in Honolulu, Hawaii, USA, May 15, 2007. The website can be found at http://p2p.ingce.unibo.it/2007/ The proceedings were published by Springer as LNCS volume no. 5319 and are available online here: http://www.springerlink.com/content/n6t202616211/

Table of Contents

Seventh Edition

Social Welfare

Altruistic Sharing Using Tags.................................... 1
  Sharmila Savarimuthu, Maryam Purvis, and Martin K. Purvis

Emerging Properties of Knowledge Sharing Referral Networks:
Considerations of Effectiveness and Fairness 13
  Priyadarshini Manavalan and Munindar P. Singh

Distributed Information Sharing

Enhancing Peer-to-Peer Applications with Multi-agent Systems 24
  Marco Mari, Agostino Poggi, Michele Tomaiuolo, and Paola Turci

Improving Self-organized Resource Allocation with Effective
Communication.. 35
  Özgür Kafalı and Pınar Yolum

Data Mobility in Peer-to-Peer Systems to Improve Robustness 47
  Hugo Pommier and François Bourdon

Network Organization and Efficiency

Trustworthy Agent-Based Recommender System in a Mobile P2P
Environment 59
  Nabil Sahli, Gabriele Lenzini, and Henk Eertink

Efficient Algorithms for Agent-Based Semantic Resource Discovery 71
  António Luís Lopes and Luís Miguel Botelho

A Semi-structured Overlay Network for Large-Scale Peer-to-Peer
Systems 83
  Kousaku Kimura, Satoshi Amamiya, Tsunenori Mine, and
  Makoto Amamiya

Eighth Edition

The Future of Energy Markets and the Challenge of Decentralized
Self-management.. 95
  Frances Brazier, Elth Ogston, and Martijn Warnier

Agent Roles for Context-Aware P2P Systems 104
   Giacomo Cabri

Working in a Dynamic Environment: The NeP4B Approach as
a MAS 115
   *Sonia Bergamaschi, Francesco Guerra, Federica Mandreoli, and
   Maurizio Vincini*

Agents and Peer-to-Peer Computing: Towards P2P-Based Resource
Allocation in Competitive Environments 129
   Yoni Peleg and Jeffrey S. Rosenschein

A Colored Petri Net Model to Represent the Interactions between a Set
of Cooperative Agents 141
   Toktam Ebadi, Maryam Purvis, and Martin K. Purvis

Author Index 153

Altruistic Sharing Using Tags

Sharmila Savarimuthu, Maryam Purvis, and Martin K. Purvis

Information Science Department, University of Otago
Dunedin, New Zealand

Abstract. This paper discusses altruistic sharing achieved by tags in an agent society where sharing information incurs a cost and non-sharing is thus the preferred option for selfish agents. We believe that the general features of our tagging mechanism can be used to facilitate altruism and increase the overall social welfare in artificial societies. We describe our findings based on experiments we have conducted through multi-agent-based simulation of artificial societies in the context of agents playing the knowledge-sharing game.

Keywords: Tags, artificial society, cooperation, altruism, Multi-Agent Based Simulation.

1   Introduction

P2P systems are increasingly attractive due to continually improving bandwidths and processing capabilities of distributed and mobile platforms. These developments support more robust systems, since P2P systems are much less susceptible to problems associated with a single point of failure. However, one of the problems associated with open P2P systems is that the nodes might not engage in a cooperative behaviour. Cooperation of individual nodes is expected to result in greater benefit for the overall society. Altruism on the part of individual agents, if it can be induced, is an attitude that would be expected to lead to societal welfare. In this paper we have investigated a mechanism based on tags which facilitates altruism. We have modeled the nodes of a P2P system as autonomous software agents. We demonstrate how altruistic cooperation is achieved in an artificial agent society in the context of agents engaging in knowledge sharing.

Tags have been used in modeling artificial society ever since Holland used them in his echo model [1]. The tags which are used in multi-agent based simulations, though, are somewhat different from the tags used in connection with folksonomies at social networking Web sites. Those folksonomy tags are used for collaborative tagging of contents., such as practiced at YouTube [2] and CiteSeer [3], where the participants create tags based on their understanding or use of the content.

The tags we use here are different, in that they are not deposited by users with an implied meaning in a social context. The tags we use are simply markings that are "visible" to other agents and are used just for grouping purposes. Examples of these tags include birds of same feather flocking together and animals that look similar to each other coming together to form a herd. Thus the tagging mechanism that we use

D. Beneventano et al. (Eds.): AP2PC 2008/2009, LNAI 6573, pp. 1–12, 2012.

is inspired by nature, and it has been widely used to model the behaviour artificial agent societies. These tags used in artificial social simulations may go through genetic evolutionary processes, such as selection, reproduction and mutation. A straightforward way to think of these tags is to assume that they represent group names for sets of agents: agents having the same tags belong to the same group., and agents of the same group have some preference to interact with others within their group. Thus people are usually friendly to others who are similar to them (belong to the same group of interests, education, ethnicity, profession, culture, personality etc.). They choose their friends, partners based on certain similarities that are assumed to represent compatibility. We use this biologically inspired tagging model in our multi-agent-based simulation of an artificial society in order to investigate how altruism might evolve in an agent society.

Various researchers within this domain have characterized what tags are in slightly different terms. According to Riolo [4] a *"tag can be a marking, display, or other observable trait. Tag-based donation can lead to the emergence of cooperation among agents "*. According to Hales [5] *"tags are observable social cues or markers attached to agents. These tags are visible : by other agents allowing them to distinguish between agents with different tags "*. It is explained in the work of Purvis *et al.* [6] that *"tagging offers a simple mechanism that can facilitate cooperative behaviour on the part of selfish individuals. Individuals just need to like or feel comfortable interacting with other individuals who are readily observed to be like them (because they have the appropriate visual tag). This is certainly a natural phenomenon in ordinary human social intercourse."*

In this paper we develop our model for facilitating altruism based on tags in the context of knowledge sharing in social interactions. We have experimented with three kinds of scenarios to observe whether altruism evolves in those setups. First, in sharing system 1 (section 3.1), we show how sharing happens when there are *no* tags in the system. In sharing system 2 (section 3.2), we demonstrate situations in which it is advantageous to use tags to evolve and maintain altruism in the process of sharing. In sharing system 3 (section 3.3), we examine the conditions under which tags are suitable to facilitate altruism and when they are less suitable for this purpose.

2   Related Work

Altruism has been of interest to researchers in the fields of sociology, psychology and computer science [7,8]. Multi-Agent Based Simulations (MABS) provide the platform for scientists to experiment with their models. This work is an attempt to achieve altruism by using tags. Some researchers have demonstrated that altruism evolves based on kin relationship [9] or due to direct or indirect reciprocity [8].

There are a few related works in which altruism has been achieved by using tags. By playing the donation game, agents employing tagging achieved altruism in the model described by Riolo [4]. In this model, tag and tolerance values are used to form groups. The peers of the same group donate to each other when the differences between their tag values lie within the tolerance limit. Also a peer (agent) could be a member of more than one group. In that case, the agent may donate to every group member of its groups and also receive from them, and this mechanism has been shown to achieve altruism among peers.

In Hales's work [5] the M3 model is used to explain the behaviour of altruistic agents which donate resources that they don't require. The agent needs to have a matching skill in order to harvest the corresponding resource. The agents are offered a few resources. If they possess the matching skill, then they can use that resource. Otherwise they can donate it to some other agent that needs the resource, or they can discard the resource without donating. The agents have enough intelligence to find a suitable agent within their tag group that can utilize the resource, and searching is employed in this process. When a donation occurs, it incurs a cost. The tag models of Riolo [4] are used in these experiments, and it was shown that the groups which are formed with a diversity of skills had better performance.

In Nemeth's work [10], the sharing is based on proximity. Agents share their knowledge with their neighbors in the locality, and this leads to the evolutionary success in their model. The altruism here is purely based on locality, and it is neither dependent on tags nor on kinship or reciprocity.

In this paper, we describe our experiments with the concept of knowledge sharing to see how altruism evolves when tagging is employed. Our model is somewhat different from the donation game or the basic resource sharing game, because the resources can be depleted by sharing, whereas knowledge is everlasting and cannot be lost by sharing.

3   Experimental Setup

To model social behavior in the artificial society, we chose a game called the knowledge sharing game. The idea for this model came from the work of Nemeth and Takacs [10] with some modifications to it, and the operation of the game is described in section 3.1. It employs a social interaction model, where the sharing of knowledge is preferred. Non-sharing is the selfish option which benefits the individual but not the society as whole. Sharing behaviour benefits the society by spreading the knowledge. Sharing does cost the donor who shares but not the receiver who receives the benefit.

In this work 'sharing the knowledge with other peers who lack knowledge' is referred to as 'altruism'. The donation (sharing) costs the donor (not in terms of knowledge, but in terms of its 'wealth') and the donor gets nothing back as a reward/benefit. Donations reduce the score (wealth) of the donor, which can lead to the decrement of its survival and reproduction chances.

The parameters of the experiment are Knowledge (K), Sharing (S), Wealth (W) and Tag.

> o   Knowledge (K bit) could be 0 or 1. If K=1, the agent possesses the knowledge, otherwise it does not.

o   Sharing (S bit) could be 0 or 1. If S=1, the agent is willing to share, otherwise it does not.
o   Wealth (W) could be 1 or below. When the agent initially possesses the knowledge, has its Wealth set to 1.   But each time it shares the knowledge, it losses 0.1 from its wealth.
o   If tag mechanism is used, the agents will have tag values. Agents having the same tag belong to the same group.

3.1   Sharing System 1 (System with No Tags)

Note that in this experiment we are not making use of tags. In the start of the game, only 20% of the population possesses the Knowledge (K=1), and 50% of the population has the tendency to share (S=1). This is the initial set-up for all the experiments presented in this paper.

Among 100 individuals at the outset, half are altruistic (S=1), and half are not (S=0). In the total of 100 individuals initially 20 have knowledge (K=1), hence they have the wealth score of 1.0 for possessing knowledge.   This leaves the agent population with four different types of players.

1.   agents with knowledge, do share (K=1, S=1)
2.   agent without knowledge, do share (K=0, S=1)
3.   agent with knowledge, don't share (K=1, S=0)
4.   agents without knowledge, don't share (K=0, S=0)

In this game, players are randomly paired, and sharing may or may not occur. Sharing happens only when one player (player1) has the knowledge and the tendency to share (K=1, S=1) and the paired player (player 2) is without knowledge.

The player who acquires the knowledge gains the wealth score 1.0. 1.0 is the maximum value of wealth that a player can have at any time in this game.   Thus if a player once received the knowledge, its wealth value can never surpass 1.0. The player with high wealth gets to reproduce more than the player with low wealth.   Sharing the knowledge does cost the donor (0.1) in terms of its wealth.   Each time it shares, it loses 0.1 from its wealth. The receiver gets the wealth benefit (1.0) with no corresponding cost. This is different from the donation game [5], in the sense that when knowledge is shared, the donor does not loose any of her knowledge by sharing it.

From the individual agent's perspective, it is better not to share, so that it can keep its score high and increase its survival chances. But for the overall society's welfare it is good to share.

The game is played with 100 players over a duration of 1000 iterations. In each iteration every player gets to play the game once as a donor (player1) and once as a receiver (player2). After each iteration 5% of the population reproduces (has one offspring), and 5% will die. The population thus has a steady state with a value fixed at 100.   The reproduction process as the end of an iteration works in the following way.   10% of the population is picked randomly, paired and compared by wealth score.   With every pair the high scorer in wealth gets the chance to reproduce *(with a very low mutation probability 0.001)* and the low scorer dies. The offspring agent is a copy of the parent, having the same behavior of the parent (sharing bit S), but not the knowledge (K bit). All young ones are born without knowledge and with a wealth of 0.0. The new agents acquire knowledge when they interact with other agents in the population that have knowledge and also have the tendency to share their knowledge with others.

Figure 1 shows the overall knowledge (not the wealth) of the population (represented by the K line) and the sharing behaviour (the S line). The experiment starts with 20% of the agents having knowledge (K line) and 50% of them having the sharing tendency (S-line). When 50% of the population comprises sharers, the population gains more knowledge. After a number of generations (around 30-40 iterations), almost 90% of the population has acquired the knowledge. The sharing tendency starts going down as the sharers die out because of their low wealth score due to the cost of donation (0.1). The selfish non-sharers take over, and the population drifts towards non-sharing, since the non-sharers retain the maximum score. After several generations (~100 iterations), the population has few with knowledge and very few with the tendency to share. Because most of the population now has the non-sharing behavior, there is less sharing and hence a decline in knowledge (remember that offspring are born ignorant). The S line then tends towards 0. When the S line is 0, there is no sharing at all, and the 5% newborn agents that appear after each iteration cannot obtain any knowledge.

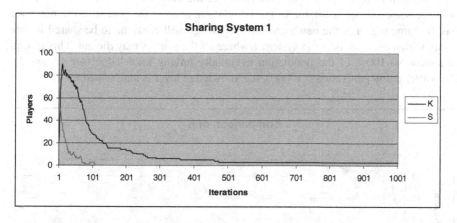

Fig. 1. The knowledge and sharing level in sharing system 1. The knowledge of the population represented by K line and the sharing behaviour by the S line.

3.2   Sharing System 2 (Tagged System)

To improve upon the scenario described in sharing system 1, we introduced a 'tagging' mechanism for sharing system 2. It has been shown to achieve cooperation in animal societies [9] and also in artificial agent societies [5, 11]. In general, most of us don't share information with just anyone, but only with those with whom we feel comfortable.

We again used the basic knowledge-sharing scenario described Section 3.1, except that there was no sharing bit assigned. Instead, the players have their group tags. The decision to share is based on tag matching. If the tags match, sharing takes place, otherwise it does not. The sharing agent's score again decreases by 0.1, every time it shares, and so sharers are more likely to die than non-sharers.

For our tag experiment, we use a string of 3 binary bits as tags (000, 001, 010, 100, 011, 101, 110 and 111). Every player is randomly assigned a tag.

When two players interact, player1 shares its knowledge with player2 if they both have the same tag. Players are altruistic towards other players who are like them (based on visual tag). 10% of the population is picked randomly, paired and compared by score. In each pair the high scorer gets the chance to reproduce and the low scorer dies so that 5% of the population reproduces in every generation. The offspring agent gets the tag of the parent (with a very low mutation probability 0.001) and has no knowledge or wealth.

This tagging makes the population of 100 players grouped into 8 tag groups (see Figure 3). These group members are always altruistic towards their own group members. Since the sharing is based on tag matching, the population keeps maintaining the knowledge by sharing it with newcomers to their group. The newborns are born with their tags which they inherit from the parent. But they have no knowledge by birth. Whenever they get to interact with other players with the same tag that have the knowledge, they receive the knowledge. Even if few players with the same tag are available in the population, at least the parent of the newborn has the same tag. For the newborns the knowledge will continue to be shared in this setup, which does not occur in system 1 where all the sharers may die out. This results in almost 90-100% of the population eventually having knowledge (see Figure 2). Even after many generations (10000), the knowledge level is maintained.

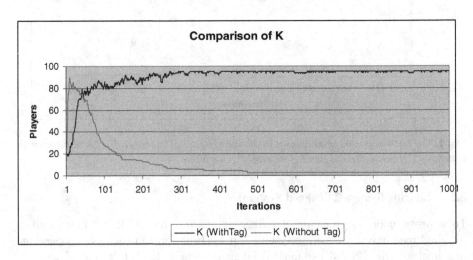

Fig. 2. Comparison of systems with and without tags

In Figure 2 the *K (without tag)* line shows the knowledge level that was achieved in sharing system 1. The *K (with tag)* line shows the knowledge achieved in sharing system 2, which makes use of tags. The tagging mechanism promotes altruistic behaviour in populations where the reward for being selfish is more than that of being fair. This mechanism does not include any direct/indirect reciprocity or any reputation/incentive mechanism or shadow of the future issues. There is no centralized control as well. And the tag groups which die out and which survive is determined here by chance. A sample experiment result is shown below (figure 3).

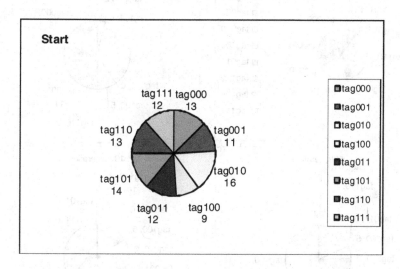

Fig. 3. 8 tag groups with different number of group members in it

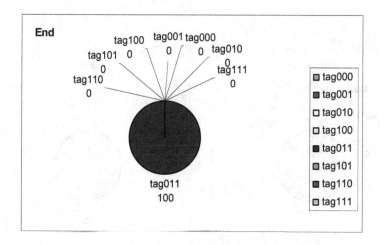

Fig. 4. Among 8 tag groups, only 1 survived and 7 died

In Figure 3 at the start of the experiment, we see 8 tag groups with varying numbers of members. In Figure 4 at the end of 1000 iterations, there is only 1 surviving group that has the entire population; others have died. In Figure 5, results showing snapshots of tag based sharing behaviour at various iteration stages are shown.

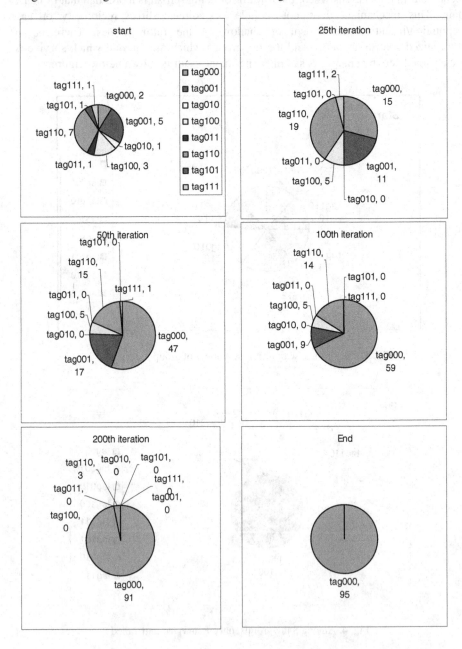

Fig. 5. Snapshots of tag based sharing behaviour at various iterations

At the outset 20 players had knowledge. When they start sharing their knowledge within their group, the number of knowledge bearers in the population increased iteration by iteration. At the end, one group ended up with all the knowledge. (Note that the maximum number of knowledge bearers in the population will be 95, because there are always 5 new agents born without knowledge.)

When we did the same experiment by varying the number of knowledge bearers in the initial population by 1, 5, 20 and 50, distributed randomly among 8 groups, the results were the same: only one group ended up with all the knowledge and survived till the end. But the rate at which the knowledge is spread is slow when the initial knowledge bearers are low.

3.3   Sharing System 3 (Hybrid System Combining System 1 and 2)

Sharing system 3 is a combination of systems 1 and 2. In sharing system 1, the decision to share is based on the S bit (if S=1) and interaction is allowed with any one in the population. In sharing system 2, the decision to share is based on tag matching and the interaction is restricted within the group. Here experimented with combining aspects of system 1 and system 2. In system 3, the decision to share is based on S bit and the interaction is local, based on tags.

We performed the experiment of sharing system 3 in essentially the same fashion as sharing system 2, with a few differences. Recall that the sharing decision in system

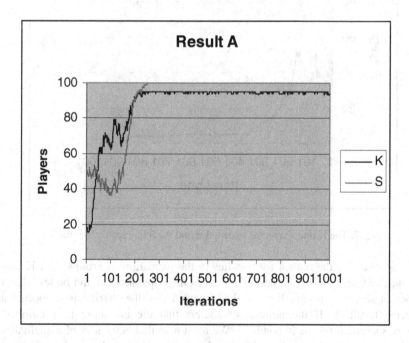

Fig. 6. The K line shows the knowledge and the S line shows the sharing

2 is just based on tag matching: if the tags matched, then the agents shared. In system 3, once the tags match, then whether sharing takes place is based on the sharing bit (S). Also, in system 2, during reproduction the offspring agents only inherit the tag of their parents. In system 3, the offspring agent also inherits the sharing tendency (S bit), as well as the parent's tag. Two sample results are given in figures 6 and 7.

In Figure 6, it can be observed that the sharers ultimately increased in numbers, so there is more knowledge-sharing in the population. Almost 95% of the population gained knowledge. Another result for the same experiment is shown in Figure 7.

In figure 7, it can be observed that the number of sharers eventually declined towards 0, and due to the lack of sharing, the knowledge level decreased.

These results that we have obtained are interesting, because we observed dramatically different behaviours for different stochastic experimental runs of the simulation. One result, call it A, shows that 100% sharing can be achieved using tags (Figure 6, see the S line), while another result, B, shows 0% sharing (Figure 7, see the S line). The probability for getting results like A over B is approximately 1/8.

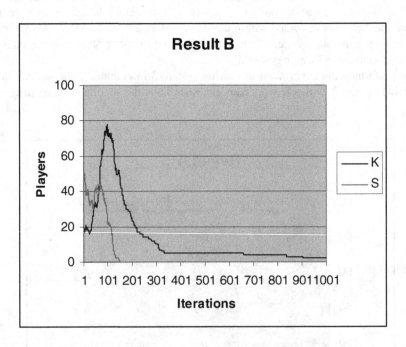

Fig. 7. The K line shows the knowledge and the S line shows the sharing

We believe that the reason for this lies in the formation of groups with K and S. The rate at which number of sharers die out in the population should be less than the number of sharers who are born in the groups. If so, the sharing is supported and produces Result A. If the number of sharers that die are more than number of newborn sharers, it results in result B. We must note that behaviour of a qualitatively similar nature was observed by McDonald and Sen [12], who explained that the number of groups invaded by defectors must be less than number of new cooperative groups formed. We are now undertaking more extensive and in-depth experiments to evaluate the implications of these scenarios. The results will be published in a forthcoming paper.

4   Conclusion and Future Work

In this paper we have shown how altruism based on tags can be used to promote improved performances for distributed P2P systems of independent agents. In the context of the knowledge-sharing game, we have shown that tagging can help sustain the knowledge possessed within the society.

From our experiments, we showed that tags do better in improving altruistic sharing when the sharing decision is just based on tag matching, when only group tags are inherited from the parents (sharing system 2). It could still fail to preserve knowledge if the sharing is based on the S-bit trait and when inheritance involves both the group tag and the sharing tendency (S Bit) as demonstrated in sharing system 3.

We note further that the experiments reported in this paper represent early stages of more extensive experimental investigations underway. There are several interesting research issues in this domain, such as a) the investigation of combining and linking tags with agent behaviour and b) investigating the relationship between the role of tag length and the size of the society.

References

1. Holland, J.H.: The Effect of Labels (Tags) on Social Interactions. Vol. SFI Working Paper 93-10-064, Santa Fe Institute, Santa Fe, NM (1993)
2. YouTube, http://www.youtube.com
3. CiteSeer, http://citeseer.ist.psu.edu
4. Riolo, R.L., Cohen, M.D., Axelrod, R.: Cooperation without Reciprocity. Nature 414, 441–443 (2001)
5. Hales, D.: Evolving Specialisation, Altruism, and Group-Level Optimisation Using Tags. In: Sichman, J.S., Bousquet, F., Davidsson, P. (eds.) MABS 2002. LNCS (LNAI), vol. 2581, pp. 26–35. Springer, Heidelberg (2003)
6. Purvis, M.K., Savarimuthu, S., De Oliveira, M., Purvis, M.A.: Mechanisms for Cooperative Behaviour in Agent Institutions. In: Nishida, T., Klusch, M., Sycara, K., Yokoo, M., Liu, J., Wah, B., Cheung, W., Cheung, Y.-M. (eds.) Proceedings of IEEE/WIC/ACM International Conference on Intelligent Agent Technology (IAT 2006), pp. 121–124. IEEE Press, Los Alamitos (2006) ISBN 0-7695-2748-5
7. Fehr, E., Rockenbach, B.: Detrimental effects of sanctions on human altruism. Nature 422, 137–140 (2003)
8. Nowak, M.A., Sigmund, K.: Evolution of indirect reciprocity by image scoring. Nature 393, 573–577 (1998)
9. Axelrod, R., Hammond, R.A., Grafen, A.: Altruism via Kin-Selection Strategies that Rely on Arbitrary Tags with which They Coelvolve. Evolution 58(8), 1833–1838 (2004)

10. Németh, A., Takács, K.: The Evolution of Proximity Based Altruism, Department of Sociology and Social Policy, Corvinus University of Budapest, Budapest (2006)
11. Riolo, R.L.: The Effects of Tag-Mediated Selection of Partners in Evolving Populations Playing the Iterated Prisoner's Dilemma, Santa Fe Institute (1997)
12. McDonald, A., Sen, S.: The Success and Failure of Tag-Mediated Evolution of Cooperation. In: Tuyls, K., Hoen, P.J., Verbeeck, K., Sen, S. (eds.) LAMAS 2005. LNCS (LNAI), vol. 3898, pp. 155–164. Springer, Heidelberg (2006)

Emerging Properties of Knowledge Sharing Referral Networks: Considerations of Effectiveness and Fairness

Priyadarshini Manavalan and Munindar P. Singh

Department of Computer Science,
North Carolina State University,
Raleigh, NC 27695-8206, USA
{ppaul2,singh}@ncsu.edu

Abstract. Referral-based peer-to-peer networks have a wide range of applications. They provide a natural framework in which agents can help each other. This paper studies the trade-off between social welfare and fairness in referral networks. The traditional, naive mechanism yields high social welfare but at the cost of some agents—in particular, the "best" ones—being exploited. Autonomous agents would obviously not participate in such networks. An obvious mechanism such as reciprocity improves fairness but substantially lowers welfare. A more general incentive mechanism yields high fairness with only a small loss in welfare. This paper considers substructures of the network that emerge and cause the above outcomes.

1 Introduction

Referral networks are a form of agent-based peer-to-peer systems [1]. Agents in such networks extensively use referrals to find other agents that can provide desired services. In knowledge-based referral networks, the focus of this paper, these services are primarily *knowledge services* [2]. For example, an agent seeking information on a subject searches for experts on the subject. Each agent maintains a set of neighbors, whom it contacts to initiate a search for experts. Unlike some conventional peer-to-peer approaches, we model the neighborhood relation as fundamentally asymmetric: Alice may not be Bob's neighbor even when Bob is Alice's neighbor. As a result, each agent can add or remove its neighbors unilaterally. Further, the in-degree of an agent may be larger or smaller than its out-degree, thus leading to interesting structures in the referral network.

Over time, as each agent finds or fails to find experts who can provide the knowledge services it requires, it may adjust its set of neighbors. The *local* adaptations of each agent cause the structure of the network to evolve. In many cases of interest, the agents evolves to form a stable network structure where most or all agents are able to obtain information more efficiently from the network. When the efficiency of individual agents in the network increases, so does the overall social welfare of the network.

In order to understand motivation behind an agent's interaction, we consider two key properties: performance and fairness. The *performance* of an agent at a specific time measures the usefulness of the surrounding network to the agent and indicates how capable the agents in the surrounding network are at providing information or referrals.

D. Beneventano et al. (Eds.): AP2PC 2008/2009, LNAI 6573, pp. 13–23, 2012.

The *fairness* experienced by an agent in a network measures how much the agent benefits from the network relative to how much work it performs.

Previous studies on referral networks focus on the properties of the network as a whole [2]. By contrast, we study the characteristics of agent interaction and have shown that in a typical referral network, performance and fairness are inversely related. This results in a structure with high agent exploitation or low performance. Autonomous selfish agents are not motivated to participate in such a setting. In addition, if we assume that most autonomous agents are selfish, their wellbeing usually takes precedence over the welfare of the network. In our study, we attempt to overcome this problem by experimenting with settings that create a network with both high performance and fairness.

Specifically, we model and consider three settings: Philanthropy, Reciprocity, and Incentives. Under *philanthropy*, our default typical network [2], agents help each other whenever they can. Under *reciprocity*, agents only help those who have helped them or whom they expect will help them. Under *incentives*, agents help others based on the incentives they receive from helping others; they can trade such incentives for their own searches, thus improving the value they obtain from the network.

Contribution. Through simulation, we find that Philanthropy is naive where although agents are successful and show high performance, the fairness of the network suffers. Some agents are heavily exploited. Reciprocity creates a fair network but the agents achieve low performance and are often unable to find the experts in the network. Incentives gets the best of both worlds: it yields fairness along with high performance.

Organization. Section 2 describes the specifics of our study, including the experimental setup and the key metrics. Section 3 describes the results of the experiments and the discussion. Section 4 concludes with a discussion of the literature and some future directions.

2   Technical Framework and Definitions

We can model a referral network as a directed graph each of whose nodes represents an agent and each of whose edges represents an agent (at the origin) having another agent (at the target) as a neighbor [3]. Each agent's *expertise* describes what knowledge it possesses and its *interest* determines what knowledge it seeks. Each agent generates outgoing queries based on its interest. Each agent may respond to an incoming query by giving an *answer* based on its expertise or a *referral* to one of its neighbors. An agent who sends out a query and receives a referral may, at its discretion, follow that referral by sending the same query to the target of the referral.

The performance of an agent reflects the good answers it can receive to its queries. Clearly, an agent's performance depends on its neighbors (modulo the setting, as we explain below). To explore the structure of the networks, we restrict each agent to have a small number of neighbors. Thus agents adapt to select neighbors that would yield them improved performance, in the process causing the network structure to evolve.

An agent's *acquaintances* are the agents with whom it has interacted. Each neighbor is also an acquaintance. Each agent maintains models that characterize the inferred expertise and *sociability* of each of its acquaintances [4]. The inferred expertise generally would not equal the actual expertise of the acquaintance. The sociability of an acquaintance corresponds to the presumed usefulness of the acquaintance in leading to a good answer to a prospective query.

Each agent evaluates the answers (if any) that it ultimately receives to its query. It upgrades the expertise of an agent that produces a good answer and simultaneously upgrades the sociability of the agents on the referral chain leading to that agent. For bad or no answers, it downgrades the expertise and sociability, respectively. Based on updates to its acquaintance models, an agent may modify its set of neighbors, in essence promoting some acquaintances to be its neighbors and demoting some neighbors to be mere acquaintances.

We use following metrics in our analysis.

- X: Set of agents
- E: The neighborhood relation
- $N_i = \{j : (i, j) \in E\}$: Set of neighbors of i
- $H_j = \{x : (x, j) \in E\}$: Set of agents of whom j is a neighbor
- $path(i, j)$: The path length of the shortest path from i to j
- I_i: The interest of agent i, modeled as a vector of dimension n
- E_i: The expertise of agent i, modeled as a vector of dimension n
- $\sigma_{j,i}$: Agent j's sociability of agent i

The similarity between two vectors of dimension n is given by

$$I \otimes E = \frac{\sum\limits_{t=1}^{n}(i_t e_t)}{\sqrt{n \sum\limits_{t=1}^{n}(i_t^2)}} \tag{1}$$

The Euclidean distance between two vectors of dimension n is given by

$$U \oplus V = \frac{e^{-\|U-V\|} - e^{-n}}{1 - e^{-n}} \tag{2}$$

The performance experienced by agent i is the summation of the contributions made by agents in the surrounding network. We define this as agents within a path of length $\log(|X|)$ from agent i. In most cases, these are the agents that provide responses to agent i. Agent j's contribution to agent i's performance is [2]:

$$\frac{I_i \otimes E_j}{path(i, j)} \tag{3}$$

The above metric reflects how similar the expertise of the agents in the surrounding network is to the agent's interest. The more similar the nearby agents are the better it is for an agent. For instance, if Agent A is interested in music and obtains high performance, this indicates that agent A's surrounding network contains experts in music.

The sociability of an agent i with respect to agent j measures i's usefulness to j. Agents that provide useful referrals tend to be rated at high sociability values and vice versa.

$$S(i) = \sum_{(j,i) \in E} (\sigma_{j,i}) \tag{4}$$

Interest Clustering measures whether the cliques formed by the agents reflect common interests among them [2]. Below $\gamma(i)$ compares i's interest with agents who are i's neighbors and have i as a neighbor. Informally, $\gamma(i)$ is high if the neighbors of i are neighbors with each other and have similar interests. Below $V_i = N_i \cup H_i$ is the set of agents that are either neighbors of i or of whom i is a neighbor.

$$\gamma(i) = \frac{\sum\limits_{(u,v) \in E} (I_u \oplus I_v)}{|V_i|(|V_i| - 1)} \tag{5}$$

PageRank measures the authority of an agent in the network [2]. An agent's PageRank depends on the PageRank of the agents of whom it is neighbor. The PageRank of each agent is divided equally among its neighbors, which makes the definition recursive. The following simplified definition of PageRank is adequate for our purposes and used to mesure authority under reciprocity.

$$P(i) = \sum_{j:(j,i) \in E} \frac{P(j)}{|H_j|} \tag{6}$$

The Relative Performance measures the benefit an agent receives as from others relative to the benefit it provides others. Below t_i and g_i are help taken and given, and equal the number of good responses received and sent, respectively.

$$R(i) = t_i - g_i \tag{7}$$

3   Experimental Results

We conducted a simulation study based on the above framework. Every agent is modeled with an interest and an expertise which remains constant over the course of the simulation. The network is seeded with each agent having some initial neighbors. Constrained only by the setting in effect, as described below, the agents generate queries in each round and exercise the referral process for each query. Therefore, we can reasonably compare the results across the three settings described below.

Philanthropy places no restrictions on an agent's interactions. Each agent always helps other agents whenever possible irrespective of how useful the other agents are to it.

Reciprocity is a variation of Philanthropy. The key difference is that, with Reciprocity, each agent helps only those agents in the network that have been helpful to it in the past or have high PageRank (which we use as a surrogate for reputation). Reciprocity ensures that agents who do not contribute to others eventually ceases to benefit from others.

If reciprocity is applied myopically, it has the risk of leading to agents not helping each other [5], because one failure by one agent to help a second agent is enough reason for the second agent to stop helping the first. To prevent this, we have each agent maintain the prospective value of each of its acquaintances. This value is adjusted upward based on good responses and downward based on bad responses. Each agent classifies its acquaintances into three primary groups and interacts with each group differently.

- High value. The agent responds to queries from high-value agents with direct responses if possible or referrals.
- Medium value. New acquaintances often fall into this category. The agent provides referrals but not answers.
- Low value. The agent disregards their queries unless they provide a referral from one of the agents' neighbors, in which it responds as usual.

Incentives is based on the idea—thinking of the incentives in monetary terms—that each agent pays for each response it receives. Each agent begins with a fixed endowment. But since each agent needs money to conduct a search, agents who help others continue to have funds to search, whereas agents who are not helpful eventually exhaust their endowments.

For a referral, an agent pays based on the quality of response received from the referral as well as the position of the referral in the referral chain. For a direct answer, the payment is predetermined. If two agents provide the same response, the response with the shorter referral chain is chosen. If this is not possible, the agent computes the similarity between its interest and the responding agent's expertise and chooses the response from agents with higher similarity. This is the same method adapted when agents do not have sufficient money to purchase all the responses received.

3.1 Agent Performance

We analyzed the outcomes of performance and fairness in a referral network based on three settings introduced above.

We expect that, as agents interact more in the network, their local performance increases and they locate the experts in the network. Moreover, the performance of an agent directly affects the manner in which the agent interacts and determines how its surrounding network evolves.

Figure 1(a) compares the performance of agents in the three different environments. Philanthropy yields higher local performance for most agents interacting in the network. Under Philanthropy, agents respond to each other freely. Thus each agent receives the best responses that it can from its surrounding network. Additionally, the number of interactions in the network is high.

Figure 1(a) also shows that under Reciprocity, the performance of each agent is significantly lower because fewer interactions take place. This is especially so for agents who do not contribute to the network.

Under Incentives, the number of responses an agent receives is proportional to the number of responses it gives. This is as in reciprocity. However, the agents don't need to have reciprocally matching interests with another agent in order to help them. The incentives can be traded in for responses from any agent. The agents, therefore have higher performance than when they are in a network defined with Reciprocity.

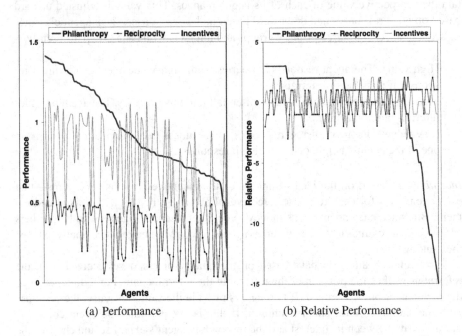

(a) Performance   (b) Relative Performance

Fig. 1. Performance and fairness for a network of 100 agents; the X axes are agents sorted best to worst with respect to the Y axis for Philanthropy

3.2 Agent Performance and Clustering

The agents that have low performance are those that show high interest clustering and high cliquishness.

Figure 2(a) shows a common network structure for a low performing agent, called A. Network structures like these evolve over the course of the simulation if agents B, C, and D have similar interests as agent A. The interest clustering for agent A is high because the neighbors of agent A also have A as a neighbor. Moreover, A has a small surrounding network. The number of agents that are a distance of one from agent A is the same as the number of agents that are a distance of two from it. Therefore, the number of agents that A can reach is small and does not increase much over the course of the simulation. The diminished size of the surrounding network causes a drastic reduction in A's local performance.

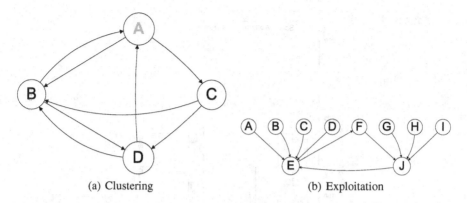

(a) Clustering   (b) Exploitation

Fig. 2. Understanding the effects of Philanthropy: (a) Low performing agents show high interest clustering and cliquishness; (b) Situations where agents are exploited

3.3 Fairness

The net benefit perceived by an agent is measured as relative performance: the number of responses the agent receives minus the number of responses it produces. A fair network is one in which all agents are treated fairly. That is, their relative performances are not widely distributed, which means each agent obtains a relative performance that is close to zero. An unfair network means that some agents are being exploited—they are the ones who do more work than they receive.

Under Philanthropy, agents may not receive sufficient help from the others. An agent may receive few or no responses, or responses of poor quality. Figure 1(b) depicts that, under philanthropy, over 20 percent of the agents in the network obtain low relative performance compared to other agents. This is depicted by the spread of the data points. In our simulation, relative performance ranges from -15 to +5. High negative values point to agents who are performing more work than they receive in the network. These agents are primarily those with high expertise values or high sociability values. Other agents gravitate toward them. As the exploitation of the agents increases, it leads to an additional problem in the network—the formation of bipartite graphs similar to the one shown in Figure 2(b).

Figure 1(b) shows that Reciprocity and Incentives result in a fair network. The range of the relative performance of the agents in the network is closer together on the vertical axis. The difference between the fairness values of both settings are very small. This is because both Reciprocity and Incentives control agent interaction and this enforces fairness. With Reciprocity, an agent only responds to those agents that have been helpful to it in the past and the responses given are usually good. Any agent that is not helping others receives limited help from others. No agent is exploited excessively. Under incentives, each agent that does not answer questions cannot ask any in return.

While Reciprocity and Incentives both result in a fair network, the number of interactions in the two models are significantly different. Reciprocity has the effect of reducing interactions. This results in formation of disjoint groups of agents. Over time, the cliquishness of the network can become much more pronounced than under

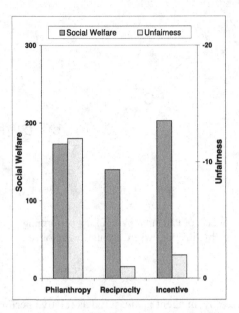

Fig. 3. Social welfare and Unfairness: for Philanthropy, Reciprocity and Incentives respectively

Philanthropy. We observe that often the network splits into disconnected components. This is because agents choose to help only a select number of agents in the network.

The *social welfare* of a network is the summation of good responses received by all agents in it. Figure 3 compares the three settings in terms of Social Welfare. Under Philanthropy, every agent answers queries even from agents that have never helped it and therefore, Social Welfare is high. Under Reciprocity, Social Welfare is significantly lower than the other two settings. This is caused by the reduced interactions. Under Incentives, agents may ask questions as long as the they have money. As the agents find the experts in the system, they can obtain responses for a cheaper rate since the referral chains for the responses are shorter in length. Therefore, they pay less for referrals and this increases the number of questions that can be asked and therefore, the Social Welfare increases too.

When social welfare is compared with the degree of unfairness as in Figure 3 in the network, the incentive model emerges as superior in referral networks.

3.4 Performance and Fairness of Expert Agents

Fairness and Performance is specially important for experts in the network. These are the most valuable agents in our network and without their participation, the efficiency of the entire network would fall. The performance of the experts varies under the three settings. Figure 4(a) shows the performance of the top twenty experts under each setting. Most experts perform best under Incentives, in the middle under Philanthropy, and worst under Reciprocity. Under Incentives, as experts provide answers, they earn money and can ask more questions. Consequently, experts interact more and are able to receive a larger number of responses than the nonexperts. However, it is interesting to note that there are a small number of experts who are different. These experts show higher performance under a Philanthropic setting than an Incentive based one. In both Philanthropy and Incentives, the contribution of these agents to the network does not alter. However, they have an added advantage in the Philanthropic network since they benefit from their neighbors being exploiters and therefore indirectly exploit other experts themselves.

Additionally, figure 4(b) shows the relative performance of these agents. Since the dispersion of relative performance of the expert agents is low, we can conclude that they perform much better in terms of fairness with Reciprocity and Incentives, than Philanthropy. Agent exploitation has been significantly reduced. Therefore, autonomous agents who are classified as experts would prefer to participate in a Incentive setting as opposed to a Philanthropic one.

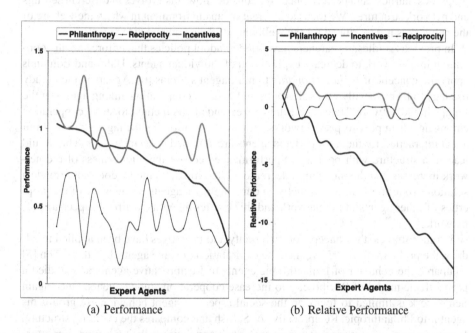

(a) Performance   (b) Relative Performance

Fig. 4. Performance and Relative Performance for a network of 100 agents: (a) Performance of top 20 experts sorted best to worst for Philanthropy; (b) Relative Performance of top 20 experts sorted best to worst for Philanthropy

4 Discussion

Philanthropy results in networks where on average the agents perform well. However, the fairness of the network is reduced and, in particular, the experts are exploited. This often results in bipartite communities.

Reciprocity results in a network that shows high fairness but low social welfare. A fundamental shortcoming of Reciprocity is that it deals only with two-party interactions. For instance, if agent A fails to help agent B, the interactions between the two would mostly not proceed (unless there is a referral from another party). In other words, Reciprocity works best when two agents are such that each can help the other. Since such pairs of agents may be rare, a lot of potential social value is lost.

By contrast, Incentives naturally supports "trade" between multiple parties. This is why Incentives yields the best of both worlds. Under Incentives, we obtain networks with high agent performance. In particular, we find that experts perform well without being exploited.

4.1 Literature Review

Yolum and Singh [2] studied the emergent properties of referral networks with respect to the policies of agents for giving referrals or answers. Here we focus on the two properties, fairness and performance. We consider how this evolves in different settings and network structures. We focused on creating an environment in which the welfare of the network is not sacrificed for the wellbeing of the agent and vice versa.

In previous studies, researchers have tried to adopt policies that enforce agent cooperation in a network to decrease exploitation of individual agents. Hales and Edmonds apply the concept of *social rationality* to multiagent systems [6]. Agents in their study use tags to form socially rational groups and enforce cooperation among agents in the groups in the network. Hales and Edmonds extended this method to study cooperation among agents in peer-to-peer networks. However, by enforcing the tag system we limit agent interaction for the most part and agents are confined to social groups. This would lead to a structure with poor agent performance because the cliquishness of the network increases and the interaction decreases. Therefore, this model does not provide a solution to our problem. Additionally, in our simulation agents are unaware of the properties of other agents in the network and this creates an entirely different peer-to-peer network.

In other studies, the concepts of reciprocity and incentives have been applied to address the problem of *free riding*, i.e., the exploitation of some agents by others. Sen [5] compared the behavior of Philanthropic agents to Reciprocative agents and studied a probabilistic model of Reciprocity to increase cooperation among agents. Once again Sen's work is limited to focus on the social aspect of agent behavior. He groups his agent into Philanthropic, Reciprocative or Selfish and compares the evolving structure. In comparison, we assume that agents are selfish and their wellbeing is more important that that of the network. We do not try to create a system of social cooperation but instead create a system where efficient agent interaction will lead to social welfare as a by product.

Yu and Singh [7] studied a dynamic pricing mechanism with the focus of studying the properties of incentive based models. In our simulation, we keep our incentive mechanism as basic as possible with fixed pricing policies. In addition, we only focused on how this mechanism affects the performance of agents with respect to fairness.

As a variety of policies based on Reciprocity and Incentives have been successfully applied to the problem of agent exploitation [5,7,8,9] in previous studies, we chose to adopt similar mechanisms in our simulation too. We adopted a simple asymmetrical referral network setting based on these policies and focused on creating, not only a fair network but also an effective one.

4.2 Future Work

This paper has opened up several interesting problems. In future work, we will study different types of incentives, including a credit-based system that reveals further characteristics of agent interactions. We will consider mixed settings where different agents may follow different settings. The results of this paper indicates that results would improve if the agents reasoned based on the incentives to provide more referrals and increased the number of their interactions. Accordingly, we will study settings where we can incorporate strategic reasoning by the agents to maximize the incentives they obtain.

References

1. Foner, L.: Yenta: A multi-agent, referral-based matchmaking system. In: Proceedings of the 1st International Conference on Autonomous Agents, pp. 301–307. ACM Press, New York (1997)
2. Yolum, P., Singh, M.P.: Emergent properties of referral systems. In: Proceedings of the 2nd International Joint Conference on Autonomous Agents and MultiAgent Systems (AAMAS), pp. 592–599. ACM Press, New York (2003)
3. Singh, M.P., Yu, B., Venkatraman, M.: Community-based service location. Communications of the ACM 44, 49–54 (2001)
4. Yu, B., Singh, M.P.: Searching social networks. In: Proceedings of the 2nd International Joint Conference on Autonomous Agents and MultiAgent Systems (AAMAS), pp. 65–72. ACM Press, New York (2003)
5. Sen, S.: Reciprocity: a foundational principle for promoting cooperative behavior among self-interested agents. In: Proceedings of the 2nd International Conference on Multiagent Systems, pp. 322–329. AAAI Press, Menlo Park (1996)
6. Hales, D., Edmonds, B.: Evolving social rationality for MAS using "tags". In: Proceedings of the 2nd International Joint Conference on Autonomous Agents and MultiAgent Systems (AAMAS). ACM Press (2003) (to appear)
7. Yu, B., Singh, M.P.: Incentive mechanisms for peer-to-peer systems. In: Proceedings of the 2nd International Workshop on Agents and Peer-to-Peer Computing (2003)
8. Krishnan, R., Smith, M.D., Telang, R.: The economics of peer-to-peer networks. Working paper, Carnegie Mellon University (2002)
9. Golle, P., Leyton-Brown, K., Mironov, I.: Incentives for sharing in peer-to-peer networks. In: Proceedings of the 3rd International Conference on Electronic Commerce (EC), pp. 264–267 (2001)

Enhancing Peer-to-Peer Applications
with Multi-agent Systems

Marco Mari, Agostino Poggi, Michele Tomaiuolo, and Paola Turci

Dipartimento di Ingegneria dell'Informazione, Università degli Studi di Parma,
Parco Area delle Scienze 181/A, 43100, Parma, Italia
{mari,poggi,tomamic,turci}@ce.unipr.it

Abstract. This paper copes with the problem of integrating peer-to-peer and multi-agent systems for the realization of both large-scale multi-agent systems and sophisticated peer-to-peer applications. In particular, it presents how JADE, one of the best known and most used software framework for the development of multi-agent systems, has been extended with a peer-to-peer technology, and how a JADE multi-agent system can be overlapped over a peer-to-peer system to provide more sophisticated services.

Keywords: JADE, JXTA, Gnutella, information sharing.

1 Introduction

Peer-to-peer and multi-agent systems have emerged as an alternative to traditional client-server systems as they can enable highly scalable end-to-end applications. However, while peer-to-peer systems have a large visibility and are widely known thanks to the applications they support, multi-agent systems are still a niche technology known and used by a restricted number of researchers and system developers.

Peer-to-peer and multi-agent systems should not be considered as an alternative since the powerful synergism between these two technologies could be very promising. In fact, while the realization of multi agent systems on the top of peer-to-peer technologies simplifies the realization of large scale-applications, the autonomy, social and proactive capabilities of agents enables the realization of more sophisticated peer-to-peer applications [Overeinder et al., 2002; Willmott et al., 2004; Buford & Burg, 2006].

This paper also copes with this problem and, in particular, presents how JADE, one of the best known and most used software framework for the development of multi-agent systems [Bellifemine et al., 2001; JADE, 2008], has been extended with a well-known and used peer-to-peer middleware, i.e., JXTA [JXTA, 2008], and how a multi-agent system can be overlapped over a peer-to-peer system to provide more sophisticated services. The next section describes in details how JXTA middleware has been integrated in the JADE software framework and how multi-agent systems realized with JADE can interoperate with systems realized with a peer-to-peer technology. Section 3 presents an information sharing application leveraging on the integration between JADE and JXTA.. Finally, section 4 concludes the paper.

D. Beneventano et al. (Eds.): AP2PC 2008/2009, LNAI 6573, pp. 24–34, 2012.

2   Coupling Multi-agent Systems with Peer-to-Peer Technologies

The traditional client-server model describes systems where computational resources and data are centralized in few servers, which respond to requests of clients. On the other hand, clients are supposed to have little capabilities and rely on the resources of servers for most of their tasks. The multi-agent model reverses this paradigm and describes systems organized in a peer-to-peer fashion, where each participant potentially has some resources to share and some services to offer to the community of agents. Thus, according to the context, each agent is able to play either the role of client or server.

JADE implements FIPA specifications for multi-agent systems, and so enables the realization of peer-to-peer distributed systems, constituted by smart and loosely coupled agents communicating by means of asynchronous ACL messages [FIPA. 2000].

Nevertheless, JADE does not exploit some important features of modern peer-to-peer networks, in particular:

1. The possibility to build a completely distributed, global index of resources and services, without relying on any centralized entity.
2. The possibility to build an "overlay network", hiding differences in lower level technologies and their related communication problems.

Some multi-agent systems, like Agentscape, approached the same issues by developing a dedicated peer-to-peer network layer [Overeinder et al., 2002]. As shown in Fig. 1, for JADE we choose to integrate agent platforms into an already existing and used peer-to-peer environment like JXTA [JXTA, 2008], thus, benefiting from a well tested system and exposing services to other entities participating in the network.

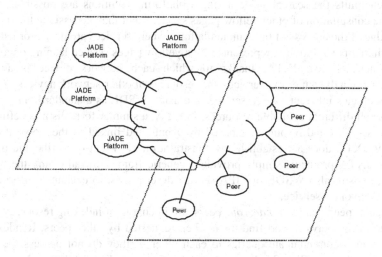

Fig. 1. Integration of JADE platforms into a JXTA network

JXTA technology is a set of open, general-purpose protocols that allows any connected device on the network (from cell phones to laptops and servers) to communicate and collaborate in a peer-to-peer fashion. The project was originally started by Sun Microsystems, but its development was kept open from the very beginning. JXTA comprises six protocols allowing the discovery, organization, monitoring and communication between peers. These protocols are all implemented on the basis of an underlying messaging layer, which binds the JXTA protocols to different network transports.

JXTA peers can form peer groups, which are virtual networks where any peer can seamlessly interact with other peers and resources, whether they are connected directly or through intermediate proxies. JXTA defines a communication language which is much more abstract than any other peer-to-peer protocol, allowing to use the network for a great variety of services and devices. A great advantage of JXTA derives from the use of XML language to represent, through structured documents, named *advertisements*, the resources available in the network. XML adapts without particular problems to any transport mean and it is already an affirmed standard, with good support in very different environments, to structure generic data in a form easily analyzable by both humans and machines.

2.1   JXTA-ADS

What usually happens in a multi-agent platform is the cohabitation of multiple agents interacting in a common and cohesive environment, making use of a formal communication language, defined by its own syntax and semantics, in order to complete tasks demanded by users. For the communication to be constructive, it is necessary to provide agents with a system allowing them to reciprocally individuate offered services. This happens thanks to the presence of a yellow pages service, provided by the platform, which can be consulted by agents when needed. However this often limits the search inside a single platform. Solutions are possible, which allow the consultation of other yellow pages services, but they necessitate the *a priori* knowledge of the address of the remote platform where services are hosted or listed.

An alternative solution is represented by a yellow pages service leaning on a peer-to-peer network like JXTA, thanks to which each network device is able to individuate in a dynamic way services and resources of other network devices.

Technologies inherent to web services are using WSDL as a standard language to publicize all different available resources. In FIPA, a simpler formalism is defined to describe services and resources exposed by agents and linked to their own domain ontology. JXTA does not establish any constraint on the way to describe and invoke services. JXTA protocols simply provide a generic framework, allowing the use of any mechanism, also WSDL or FIPA service descriptions, to exchange information needed to invoke a service.

Particular peers, called *rendezvous* peers, are in charge of indexing resources made available in the network and find them when requested by other peers. Rendezvous peers can also communicate queries to each other, if they do not possess the right information, thus enabling the discovery of advertisements beyond the local network.

In fact, in JXTA, resources are described by *advertisements*, which are essentially XML documents collecting metadata of available resources. Advertisements are not stored on some single machine, such as a server, or on a hierarchical infrastructure. They are distributed among rendezvous peers, which implement a distributed algorithm, called *shared resource distributed index* (SRDI), for the creation and management of the index of resources available in the network. On the basis of some indexed attributes, the mechanism can solve queries made anywhere in the rendezvous network. Basically, the global index is a loosely consistent distributed hash table, where the hash of an indexed attribute is mapped to some peer responsible for storing the actual advertisement.

FIPA has acknowledged the growing importance of the JXTA protocols, and it has released some specifications for the interoperability of FIPA platforms with peer-to-peer networks. In particular, in [FIPA, 2003] a set of new components and protocols are described, to allow the implementation of a DF-like service on a JXTA network. These include:

- *Generic Discovery Service* – a local directory facilitator, taking part in the peer-to-peer network and implementing the Agent Discovery Service specifications to discover agents and services deployed on remote FIPA platforms working together in a peer-to-peer network.
- *Agent Peer Group* – a child of the JXTA Net Peer Group that must be joined by each distributed discovery service.
- *Generic Discovery Advertisements* – to handle agent or service descriptions, for example FIPA df-agent-descriptions.
- *Generic Discovery Protocol* – to enable the interaction of discovery services on different agent platforms. It's a request/response protocol to discover advertisements, based on two simple messages, one for queries and one for responses.

The JADE development environment does not provide any support for the deployment of real peer-to-peer systems because it only provides the possibility of federating different agent platforms through a hierarchical organization of the platform directory facilitators on the basis of a priori knowledge of the agent platforms addresses. Therefore, at the University of Parma the JADE directory facilitator has been extended to realize a peer-to-peer network of agent platforms thanks to the JXTA technology [JXTA, 2008] and thanks to two preliminary FIPA specifications for the Agent Discovery Service [FIPA, 2003] and for the JXTA Discovery Middleware [FIPA, 2004].

This way, JADE integrates a JXTA-based Agent Discovery Service (ADS), which has been developed in the respect of relevant FIPA specifications to implement a GDS. Each JADE platform connects to the Agent Peer Group, as well as to other system-specific peer groups. The Generic Discovery Protocol is finally used to advertise and discover agent descriptions, wrapped in Generic Discovery Advertisements, in order to implement a DF service, which in the background is spanned over a whole peer group.

2.2   JXTA-MTP

In the course of some large projects based on agent technologies like Agentcities and @lis TechNet [Poggi et al., 2004; @lis TechNet, 2008], some recurring problems emerged at the level of connection among remote platforms. The importance of these problems invariably grows with the cardinality and geographical extension of the interconnected infrastructure, and has been acknowledged in other similar large scale environments.

Most peer-to-peer networks specifically address this kind of problems allowing the connection of peers located behind firewalls, Network Address Translators (NATs) and Dynamic Host Configuration Protocol (DHCP) servers, or requiring different and particular protocols like HTTP or WAP. To this end, peer-to-peer networks create an overlay infrastructure above underlying diverse and problematic links in order to realize a more abstract and homogeneous ground and simplify the communications among peers.

JXTA is one of the most used technologies to improve connectivity on a global scale. In fact, JXTA does not suppose a direct connection is available between all couple of peers. Peers can use the *Peer Endpoint Protocol* to discover available routes for sending a message to a destination peer. Particular peers, called *routers*, are in charge of responding to such queries providing route information, i.e. a list of *gateways* connecting the sender to the intended receiver. A gateway acts as a communication relay, where messages can be stored and later collected by their intended recipient, overcoming problems related to limited connectivity.

JADE, on the other hand, offers an extensible mechanism for the transport of messages among platforms, in the form of pluggable Message Transport Protocols (MTPs). The default implementations are based on IIOP and HTTP, which are both limited by the requirement of a direct connection between sender and receiver.

Exploiting the extensibility of JADE platforms, a JXTA-MTP has been developed at the University of Parma, which overcomes these limitations. To transport messages between two platforms, the new MTP uses JXTA pipes which are dynamically bound to specific endpoints (typically an IP address and a TCP port). JXTA pipes are advertised on the network in the same way as other services offered by peers, and provide a global scope to peer connectivity.

The JXTA-MTP implementation allows using not only plain JXTA pipes, but also secure ones with encryption and signature mechanisms guaranteeing privacy, integrity and authenticity of exchanged messages.

3   An Agent-Based and Peer-to-Peer Information Sharing System

We think that the file-sharing approach of actual peer-to-peer networks is inadequate when applied to documents that can not be completely described by their title or some associated metadata. On the other hand, sharing such documents would be an interesting application in various contexts, but current tools do not provide the required features for a true content sharing approach. When we refer to "*content sharing*", we mean the capability to share documents in a peer-to-peer network with the search power of a desktop search application. Therefore, we refer to the meeting point between peer-to-peer and desktop search applications, taking into consideration the advantages of each approach: the distributed file sharing of the former and the indexing capabilities of the latter.

3.1   Distributed Desktop Search

The first system we developed to test the capabilities of a content sharing application was the Distributed Desktop Search. The Distributed Desktop Search integrates the indexing capabilities of Google Desktop Search with the widely diffused Gnutella p2p network. We decided to develop the Distributed Desktop Search on an existing Gnutella client, in order to speed up the development and take advantage of all the features already included in the client. Among the available clients we chose Limewire [Limewire, 2008]. Limewire is a widely used Gnutella client entirely written in Java and it is released in a commercial and in an Open Source version, provided with a GNU GPL license.

The result of our design choices is a client that seamlessly connects to the Gnutella network and behaves like a Limewire client. It is not a simple demo application or a proof of concept, but a stable and ready-to-use software: it is released with an Open Source GPL licence and the project is hosted at SourceForge, with a download page and a dedicated Web site [Distributed Desktop Search, 2007; Mari et al., 2006].

3.2   Information Sharing

While the Distributed Desktop Search represents the application of the content sharing concept in a wide peer-to-peer network, our efforts are directed mainly toward smaller communities. Such communities have different needs in terms of security and trust delegation, and might require advanced features like the pushing of information and the support for remote users. The need for these further features brought us to put forward a new approach, i.e. *"information sharing"*, as the next step in the development of *content sharing* applications.

The first building block necessary to develop information sharing applications is the availability of a custom desktop search software. We developed a complete desktop search solution starting from the well-known Lucene [Lucene, 2003] indexing technology, together with Nutch [Nutch, 2005], a Lucene subproject that provides add-ons for indexing the most diffused file formats. These libraries, together with the JADE framework and JXTA technologies are the elements that compose the RAIS system.

3.3   RAIS

RAIS (Remote Assistant for Information Sharing) is a peer-to-peer and multi-agent system composed of different agent platforms connected through a network. Each agent platform acts as a peer of the system and it is based on three kinds of agents: a personal assistant, an information finder and a directory facilitator. Another agent, called personal proxy assistant, allows a user to access her/his agent platform from a remote system.

A personal assistant (PA) is an agent that allows the interaction between the RAIS system and the user. This agent receives the user's queries, forwards them to the available information finders and presents the results to the user. Moreover, a PA allows the user to subscribe her/him to be notified about new documents and information on some topics in which she/he is interested. Finally, a PA maintains a profile of its user preferences. In fact, the user can rate the quality of the information coming from another user for each search keyword (the utility of this profile will be clear after the presentation of the system behaviour).

An information finder (IF) is an agent that searches information on the repository contained into the computer where it lives and provides this information both to its user and to other users of the RAIS system. An IF receives users' queries, finds appropriate results and filters them on the basis of its user's policies (e.g. results from non-public folders are not sent to other users). An IF also monitors the changes in the local repository and pushes the new information to a PA when such information matches the subscriptions made by the user corresponding to this PA.

A personal proxy assistant (PPA) is an agent that represents a point of access to the system for users that are not working on their own personal computer. A PPA is intended to run on a pluggable device (e.g. a USB key), on which the PPA agent is stored together with the RAIS binary and the configuration files. Therefore, when the user starts the RAIS system from the pluggable device, her/his RPA connects to the user's PA and provides the user with all the functionalities of her/his PA. For security reasons, only a PA can create the corresponding PPA and can generate the authentication key that is shared with the PPA to support their communication. For a successful connection, the PPA has to send the authentication key, then the user must provide her/his username and password.

Finally, the directory facilitator is responsible for registering the agent platform in the RAIS network. The DF is also responsible for informing the agents of its platform about the address of the agents that live in the other platforms available on the RAIS network. RAIS directory facilitators are not the standard JADE yellow page services, but the enhanced version presented in section 2.2. In this way, RAIS queries are not limited to the agents of a single agent platforms, but are forwarded to all platform discovered on a JXTA network

3.4   Searching and Pushing of Information

In order to understand the system behaviour, we present two practical scenarios. In the first, a user asks her/his PA to search for some information, while in the second the user asks to subscribe her/his interest about a topic. In both cases the system provides the user with a set of related information.

In the first scenario, the system activity can be divided in four steps: i) search, ii) result filtering, iii) results sending and presentation, and iv) retrieval.

Search: the user requests a search to her/his PA indicating a set of keywords and the maximum number of results. The PA asks the DF for the addresses of available IF agents and sends the keywords to such agents. The information finders apply the search to their repositories only if the querying user has the access to at least a part of the information stored into them.

Results Filtering: each IF filters the searching results on the basis of the querying user access permissions.

Results Sending and Presentation: each IF sends the filtered list of results to the querying PA. The PA orders the various results as soon as it receives them, omitting duplicate results and presenting them to its user.

Retrieval: after the examination of the results list, the user can ask her/his PA for retrieving the information corresponding to an element of the list. Therefore, the PA forwards the request to the appropriate IF, waits for its answer and presents the information to the user.

In the second scenario, the system activity can be divided in five steps: i) subscription, ii) monitoring and results filtering, iii) results sending and user notification, iv) results presentation and v) retrieval.

Subscription: the user requests a subscription to her/his PA indicating a set of keywords describing the topic in which she/he is interested. The PA asks the DF for the addresses of available IF agents and sends the keywords to such agents. Each IF registers the subscription if the querying user has the access to at least a part of the information stored into its repository.

Monitoring and Result Filtering: each IF periodically checks if there is some new information satisfying its subscriptions. Then, the IF filters its searching results on the basis of the access permissions of the querying user.

Results Sending and User Notification: each IF sends the filtered list of results to the querying PA. The PA orders the various results as soon as it receives them, omitting duplicate results and storing them in its memory. Moreover, it notifies its user about the new available information sending her/him an email.

Results Presentation: the first time the user logs into the RAIS system, the PA presents her/him the new results.

Retrieval: in the same way described in the previous search scenario, the user can retrieve some of the information indicated in the list of the results.

After receiving the results, the PA has the duty of selecting N results to send to its user and ordering them. Since the IFs create a digest for each result sent to the PA, the PA is able to omit duplicate results coming from different IF agents. Then, the PA orders the results and, if the total number of results exceeds the user's constraint, the PA only selects the first N. The ordering of results coming from different IFs is a complex task. Of course, each IF orders the results before sending them to the PA, but the PA has not the information on how to order results from different IF agents. Therefore, the PA uses two solutions on the basis of its user request: i) the results are fairly divided among the different sources of information, ii) the results are divided among the different sources of information on the basis of the user preferences. User preferences are represented by triples of the form <source, keyword, rate> where: source indicates an IF, keyword a term used for searching information and rate a number representing the quality of information (related to the keyword) coming from that IF. Each time a user gets a result, she/he can give a rate to the quality of the result and, as consequence, the PA can update her/his preferences in the user profile.

3.5   Security

The information stored into the different repositories of a RAIS network is not accessible to all the users of the system in the same way. In fact, it is important to avoid the access to private documents and personal files, but also to files reserved to a restricted group of users (e.g. the participants of a project). The RAIS system takes care of users' privacy allowing the access to the information on the basis of the identity, the roles and the attributes of the querying user defined into a local knowledge base of trusted users. In this case, the user defines who and in which way can access to her/his information. Furthermore, the user can allow the access to unknown users enabling a certificate based delegation built on a network of the users registered into the RAIS community. In this sense, the system completely adheres to the principles of trust management. For instance, if the user U_i enables the delegation and grants to the user U_j the access to its repository with capabilities C_0 and U_j grants to the user U_k the access to its repository with the same capabilities C_0, then U_k can access U_i's repository with the same capabilities of U_j.

The security architecture, in particular, is founded on a more generic framework implementing a distributed RBAC model [Poggi et al., 2007]. SAML assertions are used to issue local names (i.e. roles) definitions, and chain of SAML documents can be used to link different local namespaces, to represent delegation chains.

3.6   Results and Future Work

Thanks to integration of peer-to-peer technologies, the application has gained both in flexibility and extensibility. The distributed index can be used to discover platforms in a global scope, but simply with a different configuration of the underlying peer-to-peer layer, the creation of smaller groups is made possible without other changes. Moreover, JXTA pipes allow remote peers to collaborate in a wide range of different situations, also when nodes are located behind proxies and firewalls.

Qualitative experimentations, carried on in a local area environment, have not shown a significant performance loss in the normal functioning of the system, using JXTA pipes instead of http connections. The search of remote platforms is performed only at startup, or on user request, and requires to wait for a configurable amount of time. A comparative and quantitative experimentation, in a wide area environment, instead, is still being carried on. It will also show the best configuration of the system, and its applicability.

Our future activities will be oriented towards the presentation of search results. At the moment, the Distributed Desktop Search follows Limewire order (e.g.: by availability, by connection quality, ...), while RAIS fairly divides the results among the different sources of information or it orders them on the basis of user's preferences. We still think that the most suitable way to present results in a *content sharing* or *information sharing* application is to order them by relevance, but this is a complex task for mainly two reasons:

- desktop search applications only provide a list of ordered results, but not the score given to each document, probably because it would reveal too much of the indexing algorithm;
- even if a score is available, it would refer to the system on which the document is located, not to the whole network.

Obviously, the use of the custom desktop search application, we developed for RAIS, could easily overcome the first problem, and thus the presentation of results can be treated as a problem of sorting a distributed and heterogeneous group of documents. Our intent is to provide our dedicated desktop search application with an algorithm for sorting an arbitrary (the total number is not predictable) list of documents distributed over a network of peers. The starting point for our research is once again Lucene, that uses a slightly modified version of the well-known TF-IDF algorithm [Lucene]. Our intent is to adapt the TF-IDF measure in order to take into consideration not only the local system but also the whole community. Such an approach should solve some relevant problems, e.g. the case in which too much secondary results hamper and slow down the score calculation. It would also be interesting to graphically present the results, disposing them in a two or three dimensional space, showing up not only their score, but also the relations that could bind different results.

4   Conclusions

This paper copes with the problem of integrating peer-to-peer and multi-agent systems for the realization of both large-scale multi-agent systems and sophisticated peer-to-peer applications. In particular, it presents how JADE, one of the best known and most used software framework for the development of multi-agent systems [Bellifemine et al., 2001; JADE, 2008], has been extended with JXTA [JXTA, 2008], and how a JADE multi-agent system can be overlapped over a peer-to-peer system to provide more sophisticated services.

Thanks to the integration with JXTA technologies, JADE platforms benefit from both an "overlay network", hiding differences in lower level technologies and their related communication problems, and a completely distributed, global index of resources and services. Besides, services provided by JADE agents may be exposed to peers based on other technologies populating the network.

Moreover, the paper introduces an example of application that takes advantage of the integration of multi-agent and peer-to-peer technologies. This application allows the sharing of information inside an heterogeneous peer-to-peer community where users can share information either through the services provided by the peer-to-peer infrastructure or through the more sophisticated services provided by the multi-agent layer. The RAIS system enhances a standard file-sharing application with the features provided by a multi-agent system (e.g., security, pushing of information), while, on the other hand, the multi-agent system takes advantage of the open and robust structure of a peer-to-peer network.

A more refined integration between multi-agent and peer-to-peer systems may be obtained by using Semantic Web techniques [Burstein et al., 2005]. In fact, such techniques may be the means for harmonising and then for improving the interoperability between the services provided by per-to-peer and multi-agent systems. Moreover, they may be the means for simplifying their integration with another set of technologies that are considered the reference technologies for the realization of business applications, i.e. the service-oriented technologies. Our future work will be oriented towards the enhancement of the JADE software framework by extending the current ontology support with Semantic Web techniques (i.e., use of OWL and related reasoning techniques) and the definition and experimentation of a shared format for the publication of peer-to-peer, service-oriented and multi-agent systems services.

References

1. @lis TechNet Web Site (2008), http://www.alis-technet.org/
2. Bellifemine, F., Poggi, A., Rimassa, G.: Developing multi agent systems with a FIPA-compliant agent framework. Software - Practice & Experience 31, 103–128 (2001)
3. Buford, J., Burg, B.: Using FIPA Agents with Service-Oriented Peer-to-Peer Middleware. In: Proc. of the 7th Int. Conf. on Mobile Data Management, Nara, Japan (2006)
4. Burstein, M.H., Bussler, C., Zaremba, M., Finin, T.W., Huhns, M.N., Paolucci, M., Sheth, A.P., Williams, S.K.: A Semantic Web Services Architecture. IEEE Internet Computing 9(5), 72–81 (2005)
5. Distributed Desktop Search Web Site (2007), http://distributed-ds.Source forge.net/
6. FIPA Specifications Web Site (2000), http://www.fipa.org
7. FIPA Agent Discovery Service Specification (2003), http://www.fipa.org/specs/fipa00095/PC00095.pdf
8. FIPA JXTA Discovery Middleware Specification (2004), http://www.fipa.org/specs/fipa00096/PC00096A.pdf
9. Genesereth, M.R.: An agent-based framework for interoperability. In: Bradshaw, J.M. (ed.) Software Agents, pp. 317–345. MIT Press, Cambridge (1997)
10. JADE Web Site (2008), http://jade.tilab.com
11. JXTA Web Site (2008), http://www.jxta.org
12. LimeWire Web Site (2008), http://www.limewire.com
13. Lucene project Web Site, http://lucene.apache.org
14. Mari, M., Poggi, A., Tomaiuolo, M.: A Multi-Agent System for Information Sharing. In: Proc. of ICEIS 2006, Paphos, Cyprus, pp. 147–152 (2006)
15. Nutch project Web Site, http://lucene.apache.org/nutch
16. Overeinder, B.J., Posthumus, E., Brazier, F.M.T.: Integrating Peer-to-Peer Networking and Computing in the AgentScape Framework. In: Proc. of the 2nd IEEE Int. Conf. on Peer-to-Peer Computing (P2P 2002), Linköping, Sweden, pp. 96–103 (2002)
17. Poggi, A., Tomaiuolo, M., Turci, P.: Using agent platforms for service composition. In: Proc. 6th International Conference on Enterprise Information Systems (ICEIS 2004), Porto, Portugal, pp. 98–105 (2004)
18. Poggi, A., Tomaiuolo, M.: XML-based Trust Management in MAS. In: Proc. WOA 2007, Genova, Italy, pp. 126–131 (2007)
19. Willmott, S., Pujol, J.M., Cortés, U.: On Exploiting Agent Technology in the Design of Peer-to-Peer Applications. In: Moro, G., Bergamaschi, S., Aberer, K. (eds.) AP2PC 2004. LNCS (LNAI), vol. 3601, pp. 98–107. Springer, Heidelberg (2005)

Improving Self-organized Resource Allocation with Effective Communication*

Özgür Kafalı and Pınar Yolum

Department of Computer Engineering,
Boğaziçi University,
TR-34342, Bebek, İstanbul, Turkey
ozgurkafali@gmail.com, pinar.yolum@boun.edu.tr

Abstract. Distributed resource allocation in multiagent systems is hard to solve. Since the allocation will be done distributively, agents are not aware of others that use the resources that they need and in what quantity. That is, because the agents do not have access to the entire list of allocations, they can attempt to use resources that are not available. One naive approach is to allow agents to try different allocations repeatedly, so that they can eventually an effective allocation can emerge. However, such a technique is difficult to succeed when the resources are scarce but the number of agents is high. An effective solution to the problem has to allow agents to self-organize intelligently rather than randomly. Accordingly, this paper proposes a communication scheme, where agents are allowed to exchange a small part of their prior knowledge with a few of the agents that they know. We study our proposed approach in relation to existing approaches in the literature and show the positive effects of communication on better resource allocation, especially when the resources are scarce and the agents have a variety of choices for allocation.

1 Introduction

In dynamic environments, entities need to coordinate to allocate resources that are necessary for their working. The resources may vary in terms of their properties and availability. The heterogeneity of the environment, the allocation parameters (capacities, available shared resources, tasks to allocate, and so on), individual requirements of the entities and computational complexities make it difficult to find an optimum allocation.

Centralized approaches designate an entity as a supervisor (i.e., manager, or scheduler) to coordinate the resource allocation for all parties [1], [2]. In such approaches, the supervisor becomes a single point of failure and a possible error in the supervisor may lead to no allocation of resources. More importantly, such approaches assume that entities in the system are willing to share their resource

---

* This research has been supported by The Scientific and Technological Research Council of Turkey by a CAREER Award under grant 105E073.

D. Beneventano et al. (Eds.): AP2PC 2008/2009, LNAI 6573, pp. 35–46, 2012.

needs and are satisfied with whatever allocation is done by the system. Obviously, this assumption does not hold in open environments.

Consequently, a more realistic approach is to model the entities as agents and design mechanisms for agents to allocate resources in a distributed manner. Such distributed resource allocation mechanisms are computationally more feasible than centralized approaches and are more appropriate in open environments. The distributed system may either allow communication between the agents or purely rely on the individual behavior of the agents. Both approaches may possibly lead to imperfect allocation results. A widely studied scenario of distributed resource allocation scheme is the following.

There are multiple servers with different resource capacities in the environment. At run time, several tasks are generated that require certain number of resources to be executed. The goal of a single agent is to select an available server with enough capacity to execute its task. In the distributed scenario, each agent does this selection on its own, and the whole allocation process is computed accordingly [3]. The intuition is that by self-organizing, agents will find (or learn about) servers that can satisfy their resource needs.

When the number of servers increases, the variety of the choices an agent can make also grows in size. This may lead to noticeable learning time extensions, which may further result in instable resource allocations for longer periods. That is, some servers can be left idle (i.e. undiscovered during execution) although they have enough capacities to serve the tasks, while other servers are overloaded. In order to overcome these problems, communication can be allowed between agents. While this may help the allocation process in short term (i.e., faster learning periods even when several servers are present), it also brings an overhead in terms of the computational resources. The management of such communications can be infeasible when the number of agents in the system is large. The solution is to use communication effectively and only when needed. That is, both the quality and the quantity of the communications are important.

In this paper, we propose a multiagent resource allocation mechanism where communication between immediate neighbors is allowed. We test our approach in environments where there are multiple servers to allocate tasks on. The single server scheme where communication is allowed between neighbors resembles the El Farol Bar problem [4], whereas the scheme with several servers is type of a multiple-choice minority game [5] where agents tend to be in the minority group when allocating a server (i.e., agent's utility is maximized when allocated server's capacity is not exceeded). We claim that with effective communication, the self-organization of the agents may further lead to better utilization of servers. As a result of this, the agents' individual utilizations will also benefit from it. We compare our approach to an existing approach in which communication is not allowed.

The rest of the paper is organized as follows: Section 2 gives an overview of the literature. Section 3 defines the problem formally and explains our approach in depth. Section 4 shows the results and observations of the experimental evaluations. Section 5 discusses this work and lists future directions.

2 Related Work

Several resource allocation approaches have been considered in the context of multiagent systems. Some algorithms rely on single server environments, some support multiple servers up to a limit, and yet others extend the multiple-choice minority games scheme. Sharing of knowledge and coordination is allowed in some approaches [6], but since it may be costly, some algorithms are based purely on the self-organization of the agents, and let the resource allocation emerge from it.

Cooperation between the agents is common among distributed resource allocation settings. No matter what the types of the tasks to be executed are (i.e., individual tasks, or group tasks to be performed by several agents), the allocation is performed better when the agents act cooperatively. When there are group tasks to be performed, some approaches prefer to assign agents special roles (i.e., managers), which in turn try to manage the allocation process [7]. In those settings, in order for a task allocation to be complete, either all the resources have to be sufficient for each task, or the task has to be left unassigned at all. Since the problem is NP-hard in nature [8], approximations are applied. A task manager, when assigned a task, tries to compute the efficiency of the task by finding the ratio of the task's utility and the resources required. Then, it offers the task to its neighbors in the order of efficiency. Each neighbor may be offered a number of tasks, it selects the one with the highest efficiency and sends a bid to the manager for that task. A manager selects the one with the sufficient resources and informs all the bidders for that task.

The task allocation scheme may even get more complicated when each group task has to be performed by several agents in cooperation. When the tasks also have time considerations, the solution may be achieved through combining search, task allocation, and scheduling as an integrated approach [9]. Search is related to finding agents that have the capability and time to execute a task. In order to ease the operation, the concept of a gateway agent (dominating nodes in the case of a graph) is proposed whose job is to keep track of a set of neighboring agents (i.e., in its territory) and be aware of their availability. Each non-gateway agent when assigned a task forwards its task to a gateway agent if it cannot execute the task itself. Task allocation is done by gateway agents. When none of the neighbors of a gateway agent can perform the task, it forwards the task to another gateway agent. It may be the case that multiple agents are found at the end of this propagation process. Then the task originator decides whom to assign the task, probably the one with an available schedule. When looking for an available schedule, the gateway agent constructs an aggregation of the time vectors of each of its neighbors. This time availability is combined with resource availability (capability of the agents) and propagated in the network.

The complication of the self-organization scheme degrades when the tasks to be allocated are simple rather than composite. One idea is to introduce algorithms to automate the neighbor selection (i.e., self-organization) in large networks of agents in order to help ease resource allocation [10]. The agents in that setting try to perform as much tasks as they can once they're assigned the tasks.

But, if that is impossible, they tend to pass them to their immediate neighbors. This cycle can continue until an agent capable of performing the job is found. Since this search is costly each time a task is assigned, it is wise for an agent to reorganize its neighbors when needed (i.e., to find the capable agents in one iteration of the search). At this point, multiagent reinforcement learning is utilized which takes into account learning from prior experience. Agents try not to lose any previously learned knowledge when reorganizing, but rather extract useful parts of it to be available in the new neighborhood. This reorganization process can also speed up with some heuristics to be employed.

Another important approach on the aforementioned setting is an extension of the El Farol Bar problem in which there are multiple servers to allocate resources [3]. Their proposed approach is purely based on the self-organization of agents, and thus does not require any manager agents to help perform the allocation process, or any exchange of information between the agents. It is then an emergent property of the system that resource allocation is performed as a result of the self-organization process. The individual behavior of the agents is based on a probabilistic approach, where each agent has a number of predictors for each server. The predictors try to forecast the availability of the servers for future allocations based on the local history of the agent's past allocations. Each predictor has a different way to compute the future availability of the server, which prevents two agents having the same allocation history to select the same server each time they try to execute a task.

The approach proposed above is shown to be effective on the resource allocation problem. But, it has certain limitations. First, the authors have experimented an environment where the total capacity of the servers is much higher than the resource requirements of the tasks to be executed. In such an environment, it is considerably easier to maximize agents' individual utilizations as well as the utilizations of the servers. The second limitation of their approach is the bound on the number of servers. They have performed their experiments with three servers only and have given an upper bound on the learning time of agents (the time until the allocation becomes stable in terms of the server capacities). When the number of servers increases, the learning time will also increase dramatically.

3 Proposed Approach

Our proposed approach extends Schlegel and Kowalczyk's approach to account for cases when the resources are scarce as well as the cases when the resources are highly distributed.

3.1 Problem Definition

Here, we describe the resource allocation problem discussed in this paper formally. The environment consists of a number of servers, each with a previously specified capacity that remains constant throughout the simulation. Accordingly, a server can be represented a two-tuple {serverName, capacity}, and for each server a history of past allocations is kept by the simulator. Besides the servers, the environment hosts the autonomous agents, which try to perform their assigned tasks on the servers depending on the resource consumption of the task. The simulation is a series of timesteps, where in each timestep the agents are assigned tasks to be executed. A task is a three-tuple {timestep, assignedAgent, resourceConsumption}. A task allocation is considered successful if the server on which the task is executed is not over-utilized in that timestep (i.e., the allocation does not exceed the capacity). The utilization of a server is computed by the simulator after each agent allocates its tasks on some servers. All allocations from agents that allocate their tasks on an over-utilized server are considered unsuccessful for that timestep. Thus, the individual utilization of an agent is a binary value (i.e., true or false) when considered for a single task.

3.2   Agent Behavior

The agent's individual behavior is based on a set of predictors designed for several tasks. Generally, there are three types of predictors an agent has: the query predictor to decide whether to send outgoing queries to other agents, an agent predictor for each agent it interacts with to decide whether the agent is trustworthy, and a set of server predictors to store the confidence value of a successful allocation for each server to decide whether a particular server should be used in future allocations.

The query predictor, when agents are allowed to communicate, is responsible for telling the agent whether to send outgoing queries or not. If the agent has previously detected a server with predicted availability value above a certain threshold, then it has no incentive to ask others for their opinions on the servers. The behavior of the query predictor is given below:

$$queryNeeded = \{ \begin{array}{l} false , serverAvailability_i \geq threshold, i = 1..numServers \\ true \ , otherwise \end{array}$$

The agent predictor, defined for each agent, stores the expertise and sociability values modeled for that agent [11]. The expertise of an agent tells how well it knows the availability of servers in the environment. This is a single averaged value, not modeled for each server separately. Likewise, the sociability of an agent is an averaged value representing the knowledge of the agent about other agents in the environment. The predictors are updated according to the information gained from corresponding agents.

The server predictors store a means of the corresponding server's availability information. It is a composite structure where the number of past allocations, their corresponding allocation results, and an averaged confidence value is kept. Each agent keeps a separate server predictor for each server it has encountered (i.e., made an allocation) before. The confidence value for a server is computed after each allocation of the agent on that server. It is an averaged value of the successful allocations over the total number of allocations made on that server.

$$ServerConfidence = \frac{\sum_{i=1}^{numAllocations} allocationResult_i}{numAllocations},$$

where *allocationResult* at timestep t is:

$$allocationResult_t = \begin{cases} 0 \text{ , allocation was unsuccessful at timestep } t \\ 1 \text{ , } otherwise \end{cases}$$

In this paper, we let the agents utilize two ways to exchange information, and a scheme where no communication occurs. Next, we will describe these different schemes.

No Communication: The agents in this approach purely rely their server selection strategy on their server predictors. That is, they use their local knowledge (i.e., past allocation history) to select a server for allocating its currently assigned task. Below, we will see how the server selection is performed (Algorithm 1):

Algorithm 1. Probabilistic Server Selection

1: **for all** *serverPredictors* **do**
2:    record the server confidence values from the predictors
3: **end for**
4: transform the recorded confidence values into a probability distribution
5: **return** the server selected according to the probability distribution

---

We extend the no communication scheme with the concept of inertia [12], the intention of the agent to stay on its last allocated server. This will be considered as a separate approach in the experiments within the no communication scheme. According to its inertia, the agent selects a server as follows (ignoring the probabilistic selection algorithm):

$$server = \begin{cases} server_i \text{ , } serverConf_i \geq tConf \text{ \& } numAlloc_i \geq tAlloc, i = 1..numServers, \\ none \text{ , } otherwise \end{cases}$$

where *serverConf* is the predicted server availability value, *numAlloc* is the past number of allocations on that server, *tConf* is the threshold value for the confidence in selecting the server, and *tAlloc* is the threshold value for the number of past allocations to pass.

Exchange Server Confidence Information: In this approach, we let the agents exchange their local knowledge of the servers' availability when requested. An agent decides whether to consult other agents about the availability of a server based on its query predictor. If the query predictor tells the agent that its local information is not enough to make a successful allocation, it prepares queries defining which agents to ask, and about which servers. On response, there are two possibilities; the consulted agent may tell the server confidence value to the requesting agent if it has previously allocated on that server, otherwise it gives the name of another agent as a referral. The agent predictors are used when deciding which agents to ask the queries. It is a probabilistic selection like the server selection algorithm which depends on the modeled expertise values of the neighbors of the agent.

Exchange Past Allocation Information: In this scenario, the agents exchange a small portion of their past allocation histories. Starting from the end of the first timestep, the neighbor agents exchange the names of their last allocated servers. This information becomes valuable when the allocation history received from an agent includes at least three timesteps. Then, the agent has a means to evaluate that information. Simply, the agent applies a penalty to its server confidence value if the received information from an agent includes that server in at least two of the last three allocations. This is proof enough to predict that agent's next allocation. The agent repeats this procedure for all of its neighbors. After the server predictors are reorganized, it selects the server to execute its currently assigned task based on the probabilistic approach explained before. The whole computation is performed as described in Algorithm 2:

Algorithm 2. Probabilistic Server Selection with Penalty

1: **for all** *serverPredictors* **do**
2:     record the server confidence values from the predictors
3:     **for all** *receivedAllocationsFromNeighbors* **do**
4:         **if** server exists at least twice in three of the allocations received from an agent **then**
5:             apply a penalty to the confidence value of the server
6:         **end if**
7:     **end for**
8: **end for**
9: transform the recorded confidence values (with penalty applied) into a probability distribution
10: **return** the server selected according to the probability distribution

---

The two same servers out of three allocations the agent uses to apply the penalty on a server is a heuristic supported by experimental simulation. We have also tried more strong proofs to predict an agent's next allocation (i.e., three out of four, etc), but it does not have an extra visible effect on improving the allocation process.

4   Experiments

We evaluate our approach in different environments to study how well the approach performs when (1) the number of resources is scarce and (2) the resources are highly distributed. To study these two properties, we have setup three sets of simulations as follows:

1. *5 servers where server capacities greatly exceed task requirements*
   In this experiment, we set the server capacities noticeably higher than the resource requirements of the tasks to be executed.

2. *5 servers where server capacities are almost equal to task requirements*
   For this experiment, we have reduced the total server capacity while keeping
   the number of servers the same (i.e., the server capacities and resources to
   allocate are almost equal in size).
3. *10 servers where server capacities are almost equal to task requirements*
   In this experiment, we keep the total server capacity the same as in the
   second experiment (i.e., scarce resources), but doubled the number of servers
   so that the resources become more distributed

In each set of simulations there are 1000 agents, and each task requires 25 resources with a deviation of ten percent to execute. So we can assume, without
loss of generality, that the required capacity for all tasks to be executed successfully is around 25000. The percentage of neighbors to the total number of
agents is one percent, thus each agent has 10 neighbors to exchange information
with. To overcome the random behavior employed by the random task generation
algorithm, we have run each simulation five times, and recorded the averages.

In each set of simulations, we change the communication scheme to see how it
affects the utilization of servers as well as agents, themselves. We have repeated
the simulations for the three agent types: no communication case, no communication where agents utilize inertia, and a communication scheme where agents
exchange past allocation information among their neighbors. We do not show
the effects of exchanging server confidence information since it does not improve
the allocations. We briefly explain why this is so in Section 5.

4.1 Metrics

The following are the metrics we have used to evaluate the approaches:

1. *Agent Utilization*
   This metric measures the average of the individual utilizations of the agents.
   Remember that the utilization of an agent depends on the binary outcome of
   its past allocations (i.e., the utilization is maximized when the selected server
   is not over-utilized). This metric is especially helpful when the server capacities are enough to detect unsuccessful allocation approaches. We compute
   the overall agent utilization as follows:

$$AgentUtilization = \frac{\sum_{i=1}^{numAgents} agentUtil_i}{numAgents},$$

   where $agentUtil$ at timestep t is:

$$agentUtil_t = \begin{cases} 0 \text{ , allocated server is over-utilized at timestep } t \\ 1 \text{ , } otherwise \end{cases}$$

2. *Deviation from Server Capacity*
   This is the actual metric that measures how successful the allocation is.
   In order to compute the overall deviation value, we average the deviation
   percentages from each server's capacity. We will be using this metric to
   compare the different self-organization approaches when the server capacities

and the task requirements are equal in quantity. The computation of the average deviation value is shown below:

$$ServerDeviation = \frac{\sum_{i=1}^{numServers} serverDev_i}{numServers},$$

where $serverDev$ at timestep t is:

$$serverDev_t = |1.0 - (allocation_t/capacity_t)|$$

4.2   Agent Utilizations When Server Capacities Are Enough

The server capacities for this set of simulations are 6000, 3500, 7000, 5000, and 8500. As we can notice the total server capacity in the environment is 30000, where the total number of resources to allocate is roughly 25000. In order to evaluate the allocation performances better, we set the server capacities much different than each other.

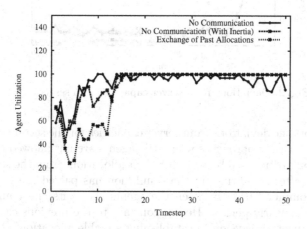

Fig. 1. Agent utilizations in 5 server case

Figure 1 plots the average agent utilizations for the first experiment. As the figure displays, the two approaches, when there is no communication but the agents utilize inertia, and the communication scheme where agents exchange their past allocations, become stable at perfect agent utilization after 15 timesteps have passed in the simulation. However, the other approach, where agents only rely on the their own predictions and always keep the probabilistic server selection algorithm does not fully stabilize. The main reason for that is the non-deterministic behavior of the agents when allocating the resources. Although there are servers that the agent strongly believes in their availability, it may still select another server with small probability. Even though the no communication case is not fully stable, its performance is still comparable to the other two approaches.

4.3   Server Utilizations When Resources Are Scarce

The total number of resources to allocate is again roughly 25000. However in this experiment, the server capacities are 4000, 3500, 6000, 5000, and 6500. So, in this experiment the total server capacity in the environment is also 25000. This setting is meant to test the performances of the approaches when the resources are scarce.

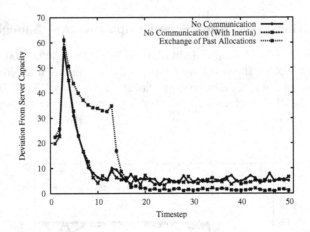

Fig. 2. Deviations from server capacities in 5 server case

Figure 2 plots the deviations from server capacities for the second experiment. Here, we see that the approaches where the agents are not allowed to exchange any information are noticeably deviating their allocations from the server capacities. However after some time in the simulation has passed (i.e., the learning period), the communication between the agents shows its effect and the allocation process is nearly perfect. Hence, contrary to the previous case, having a simple communication pays off in establishing a stable allocation.

4.4   Server Utilizations When Resources Are Distributed

The total number of resources to allocate, and the total server capacity are also equal in the last set of experiments, 25000. The server capacities are 2500, 3000, 1000, 2000, 3000, 4500, 3500, 1500, 2000, 2000. The aim of this setting is to see the effect of resource distribution.

Figure 3 plots the deviations from server capacities for the third experiment, where the number of servers is doubled. The results are nearly the same with the previous experiment. The no communication schemes again fail to provide an allocation scenario more than the emergent result of a random self-organization of agents. The communication among the agents still keeps the allocation near perfect, but this time slightly more timesteps are required to make the allocation stable. This is intuitive, since the number of servers to be learned about has increased.

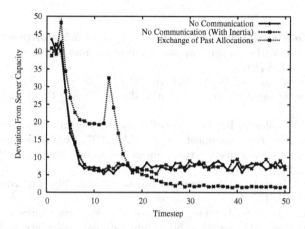

Fig. 3. Deviations from server capacities in 10 server case

5 Conclusions

In this paper, we have proposed a resource allocation approach based on the self-organization of the agents. In order to enhance the efficiency of the allocation, we allowed agents to exchange a small portion of their history. According to the results of the experiments, effective communication helps better utilize the available resources when close neighbors are allowed to exchange their past allocation choices.

During our research, we have also experimented a different type of communication between the agents as we have discussed previously. The agents were allowed to share their current knowledge about the servers' availability when requested. We have not included the results of those simulations, since that communication scheme did not have a visible effect on the resource allocation process. There are several reasons for that; one is, although the information that flows between the agents is completely true in terms of the agent's own beliefs, it may not be very helpful for the requesting agent. Because the correctness of an allocation on a server only depends on the current number of tasks executed on that server and nothing else, previously modeled availability of servers coming from another agent does not add any extra value to the agent's own model of the servers.

There are still many aspects to consider as future work. First of all, we did not consider the case where the capacity of the servers change over time during the execution of the simulation. In such a case, the reorganization process should complete in a reasonable time (i.e., relearning period), and the allocation should be stabilized again. Second, we restricted the agents to respond honestly when sharing information as done in previous research. This is not an unrealistic approach in terms of the agent's own utilizations, since the overall allocation becomes better when correct information flows in the environment. But, it may be interesting to study cases when the agents can respond untruthfully.

References

1. Foster, I., Kesselman, C.: Globus: A metacomputing infrastructure toolkit. The International Journal of Supercomputer Applications and High Performance Computing 11, 115–128 (1997)
2. Frey, J., Tannenbaum, T., Foster, I., Livny, M., Tuecke, S.: Condor-G: A computation management agent for multi-institutional grids. Cluster Computing 5, 237–246 (2002)
3. Schlegel, T., Kowalczyk, R.: Towards self-organising agent-based resource allocation in a multi-server environment. In: AAMAS 2007: Proceedings of the 6th International Joint Conference on Autonomous Agents and Multiagent Systems, pp. 1–8. ACM (2007)
4. Arthur, B.W.: Inductive reasoning and bounded rationality. The American Economic Review 84, 406–411 (1994)
5. Galstyan, A., Kolar, S., Lerman, K.: Resource allocation games with changing resource capacities. In: Proceedings of the International Conference on Autonomous Agents and Multi-Agent Systems, AAMAS (2003)
6. Rustogi, S.K., Singh, M.P.: The Bases of Effective Coordination in Decentralized Multi-agent Systems. In: Müller, J., Singh, M.P., Rao, A.S. (eds.) ATAL 1998. LNCS (LNAI), vol. 1555, pp. 149–161. Springer, Heidelberg (1999)
7. de Weerdt, M., Zhang, Y., Klos, T.: Distributed task allocation in social networks. In: AAMAS 2007: Proceedings of the 6th International Joint Conference on Autonomous Agents and Multiagent Systems, pp. 1–8. ACM (2007)
8. Shehory, O., Kraus, S.: Methods for task allocation via agent coalition formation. Artificial Intelligence 101, 165–200 (1998)
9. Theocharopoulou, C., Partsakoulakis, I., Vouros, G.A., Stergiou, K.: Overlay networks for task allocation and coordination in dynamic large-scale networks of cooperative agents. In: AAMAS 2007: Proceedings of the 6th International Joint Conference on Autonomous Agents and Multiagent Systems, pp. 1–8. ACM (2007)
10. Abdallah, S., Lesser, V.: Multiagent Reinforcement Learning and Self-Organization in a Network of Agents. In: Proceedings of the Sixth International Joint Conference on Autonomous Agents and Multi-Agent Systems, Honolulu, IFAAMAS, pp. 172–179 (2007)
11. Yolum, P., Singh, M.P.: Engineering self-organizing referral networks for trustworthy service selection. IEEE Transactions on Systems, Man, and Cybernetics A35, 396–407 (2005)
12. Rustogi, S.K., Singh, M.P.: Be patient and tolerate imprecision: How autonomous agents can coordinate effectively. In: IJCAI, pp. 512–519 (1999)

Data Mobility in Peer-to-Peer Systems to Improve Robustness

Hugo Pommier and François Bourdon

GREYC Laboratory - UMR 6072,
University of Caen Basse-Normandie,
boulevard du Marchal Juin BP 5186 - 14032 Caen CEDEX France
{hpommier,fbourdon}@info.unicaen.fr

Abstract. In this paper, we present the design of a robust decentralized peer-to-peer (P2P) platform for data storage. We use Fragmentation Redundancy and Scattering (FRS) mechanism on a file to provide fault tolerance capability, and information availability. To build a fully decentralized system, we consider each fragment of information as an autonomous bio-inspired agent capable to choose his own place of storage (to move from a peer to another peer). To reconstruct a file we have to gather a subset of fragments (defined by a minimal threshold to reconstruct the entire document), thus we have implemented flocking rules to maintain a swarm of fragments. These simple local rules allows us to find just one fragment to steer the whole flock towards a peer in the network. Another issue is the use of all network capabilities. We show in this paper how the flock mobility (based on pheromones) can provide the load distribution, while avoiding suspicious peers.

1 Introduction and Motivation

The main goal of P2P applications is to provide resources through a network for a set of peers. Millions of users use P2P applications to share data or computing resources, watch television, talk to friends across the world. All of theses services need scalability, efficient routing and localization of data. Security, confidentiality, and privacy are important problems. Servers provide these capacities but they suffer a bottleneck effect. Decentralized applications and offer same responsibilities to users solve a part of this problem, but the need for confidentiality is still present. Our work is motivated by the following fact: intercepting a data item makes it possible to obtain information about neither data's owner nor content.

In this paper we focus on these properties to provide a new approach for a robust data storage P2P platform. Here robustness means :

- **Fault-Tolerance:** Tolerate both accidental and intentional faults. Services proposed have to resist to a physical failure or a deny of service attack. Furthermore we have to take into account confidentiality attacks. Files interception should neither reveal any kind of information about contents nor his owner.

D. Beneventano et al. (Eds.): AP2PC 2008/2009, LNAI 6573, pp. 47–58, 2012.

- **Trust in Peers:** Identify suspicious nodes among all peers. Peers are able to detect doubtful behavior in the network and so prevent data storage on these nodes.
- **Information Availability:** Guarantee information durability. A regular user may accidentally erase data, or a physical failure may delete confidential files, information has to persist and to be reachable in the network.

The rest of this paper is organized as follows. We discuss related work in the next section. Section 3 and 4 shows our architecture proposition. Section 5 presents some experimental results leaded on our simulator. Section 6 presents a discussion on the applications and the evolutions of our model. We conclude in Section 7.

2   Related Work

Several decentralized data storage applications built on a self-organizing, scalable, and fault-resilient routing substrate has been proposed. PAST [1] is one of them. It allows a user to store files in a network based on the pastry [2] protocol. Strong persistence and reliability is the main goal of PAST. This is reached by storing k replicas of inserted file, while the communication layer is assured by pastry. Privacy and security of files [3] are insured by using a smartcard.

In the same way Pond [4] (the Oceanstore prototype) provides a persistent data storage. The conception of Oceanstore [5] is based on two parts. Build a network from untrusted servers and support monadic data (separation of information from its location). Files in this architecture are duplicated and encrypted to be stored on untrusted locations. Oceanstore uses erasure codes [6] to achieve fault-tolerance on data. Like PAST, Pond is upon an efficient routing layer, Tapestry [7].

Main objectives of the Freenet architecture, a decentralized peer-to-peer sharing application [8], are anonymity for both publishers and clients. This capability is provided by using cryptography on inserted data and by a probabilistic routing scheme which avoids the data storage on predictable servers. These requirements limit the global performance of Freenet. Replication is also a limitation. Data are only duplicated on a client request. Thus unpopular information are not persistent in the network.

A closer work from our is Anthill [9]. This system uses a multi-agent system, based on an ant colony, to provide a framework for P2P application development. The network consists of interconnected nests where ants are autonomous agents trying to satisfy clients requests. Ants can interact with their environment and then perform a local decision. A file-sharing application, Gnutant, has been built on anthill framework.

Majority of data-storing applications uses cryptographic methods and duplication to provide security and privacy. The research reported in this paper introduces mobility and multi-agent systems to make a peer-to-peer application safer.

3   Theoretical Background

Our architecture consists of splitting up a document, duplicating fragments and finally spreading them. The originality of our approach is to manage fragments movements with flocking rules.

3.1   Fragmentation Redundancy and Scattering

The Fragmentation, Redundancy, and Scattering [10] is a technique used to provide robustness. A sensible data is fragmented and scattered across a network to resist intrusions. Each data fragment contains no significant information on the original data. The architecture described in [11] allows a user to store sensible data in a network. The major weakness of this application is the authentication/authorization servers whose are responsible for access right checking and for giving tickets to recover the data (places where to find fragments and a fragmentation key).

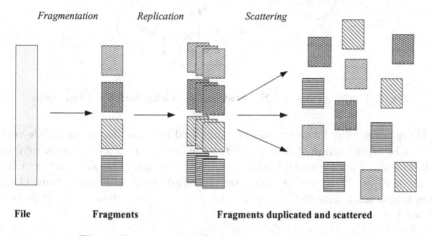

Fig. 1. Fragmentation, Redundancy, and Scattering

Decentralize a FRS architecture entails problems. Fragments randomly scattered across the network are difficult to find. So the cost to reconstruct a data is too important. To improve that, flocking rules are used to keep cohesion between fragments. This property allow to find just one fragment to reach the others. So, the data reconstruction is facilitated.

3.2   Flocking

Mobility is the main idea of our architecture. To secure a data storage application, nodes where informations are stored should stay secret. In order to decentralize a FRS application, we use a multi-agent system in which every information fragments are mobile agents making their own decisions. So, a fragment can choose the best storage location in the network. To manage the agent mobility, we use flocking rules. In [12], Craig Reynolds was interested to the phenomenon of birds flying in coordinated flocks. The challenge was to uncover simple rules that each agent must follow. That would produce flocking as an emergent behavior. In this model, flocking is not a quality of any individual bird. Reynolds identified three simple rules for each agent to follow:

1. **Separation:** Steer to avoid crowding local flockmates.
2. **Cohesion:** Steer to move toward the average position of local flockmates.
3. **Alignment:** Steer towards the average heading of local flockmates.

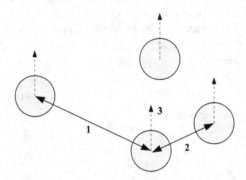

Fig. 2. Flocking rules: **1 - Separation, 2 - Cohesion, 3 - Alignment**

There are several flocking models mainly used for coordination of mobile vehicles [13,14]. Application of Reynolds's rules in our model produce a moving flock of fragments. This approach leads to many advantages. The obstacle avoidance is one of them. If suspicious nodes are identified, flock will avoid them. Gathering fragments is also facilitated. Flocking rules allow to find one fragments to attract the others.

3.3 Bio-inspired Agents: Pheromone Dropping

We also use a **pheromone** drop mechanism during the agents movements. A fragment marks his departure from a peer to another one by dropping a pheromone. It also mark his arrival by a pheromone. So this level must be equal between two peers.

Notation 1. *Let x, and y two peers. We will denote by ϕ_{xy} the pheromone level between x and y.*

We also introduce pheromones evaporation. Thus, an environment observation provide information on network traffic. A low pheromone level, for a given peer, indicate a weak activity. Thanks to this mechanism, we can build a simple measure to observe the network load, and a trust measure that allows fragments to move on safer nodes.

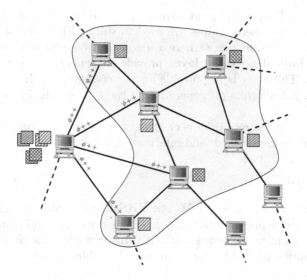

Fig. 3. Agents are scattered following flocking rules. At each movements pheromones are dropped ($\phi + +$) on both peers.

4   System Architecture

The proposed architecture is composed of three layers (fig 4). The first one is the **fragment layer**. Fragmentation and redundancy apply to a file produce fragments stored in this layer.

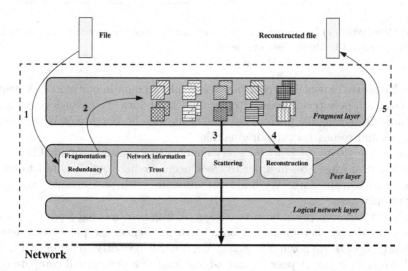

Fig. 4. Layered model. (**1**) A document is inserted, (**2**) fragmented and duplicated. (**3**) Agents are scattered. (**4 and 5**), fragments are gathered and merged.

The secondary layer is the **peer layer**. FRS, and trust establishment mechanisms are performed here. Tables are used to store all information relative to the network. It is also the place where a fragment choose his next destination.

Finally the **logical network layer** provide elements to the communication between peers. This layer is responsible for the creation and the update of the neighborhood. All information generated by these protocols are stored in the peer layer.

We are now going to retail the peer layer. This is the location where trust is established, moves are decided, and information are stored.

4.1   Peer Layer

This layer contains two units (fig 5). The **FRS mechanisms** is responsible for fragmentation and replication of a file. Flocking rules are applied in the movements block to manage fragments scattering. **Information block** maintains up to date information related to the network and establishes trust.

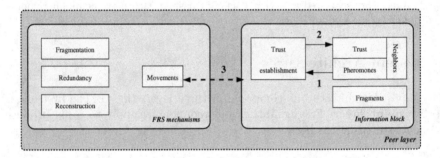

Fig. 5. Peer layer. (**1**) Information in the pheromone table are gathered, (**2**) the trust table is updated. (**3**) Movements are decided.

Trust Measure. Suspicious peers are taken into account in our model. A suspicious node is a peer trying to intercept confidential data. The attack consists in artificially decreasing the pheromone level in its neighborhood to attract moving fragments and reconstruct the original file.

Peers can evaluate the trust for every member in its neighborhood. This measure evaluate storage sites in order to track peers having suspicious functioning, or trying to corrupt data. We build this measure with pheromones deposited along the network.

Each link between peers have two ways. A fragment moving from a peer to another one drops pheromones on both of them. Hence, the pheromone levels between two peers are normally equals. We use this property to propose a trust establishment scheme. A peer x establishing trust of a peer y, will compare ϕ_{xy} and ϕ_{yx}. If there is a difference x request two neighbors of y to validate the behavior of y. Algorithm 1 provides a such measure.

Algorithm 1. Trust establishment algorithm for a peer x to a peer y

---

Input: A peer y, ϕ_{xy}
Output: Trust for peer y
x request ϕ_{yx} to y;
if $\phi_{xy} \neq \phi_{yx}$ **then**
  | x chooses two neighbors of y (Peer 1 and Peer 2) in its neighborhood;
  | x request ϕ_{1y} and ϕ_{2y};
  | x request ϕ_{y1} and ϕ_{y2};
  | **if** $\phi_{y1} \neq \phi_{1y}$ *or* $\phi_{y2} \neq \phi_{2y}$ **then**
  | | x decrease trust in y;
  | **else**
  | | x increase trust in y;

else
  | x increase trust in y;

The main advantage of this algorithm, based on Byzantine agreements [15,16], is to measure the trust in a neighborhood only by observing the peer environment. There is limited information exchange, thus the risk of corruption of a such measure is very low.

Fragmentation, and Redundancy. The fragmentation must ensure that no useful information can be obtained from isolated fragments. Therefore all the fragments must have the same length and their names should not reveal any information. To perform fragmentation we can use a scheme based on erasure codes, similar to Oceanstore [4]. Erasure codes are used to share a secret [17] by dividing a block into m identically-size parts, which are then encoded into n fragments. The main property of erasure codes is that the original block can be reconstructed from n fragments.

In addition to fragmentation, we introduce redundancy. Each fragment is duplicated in order to provide data availability. If a user wishes maximum robustness, the number of replicas have to be the lowest. In the opposite a higher degree of replication provide a better availability but more fragments are exposed to suspicious users. The replication degree is important and has to be relied to the fragment number.

Scattering (Flocking). The last operation is agents scattering. [10,11] broadcast fragments replicas to storage sites. A temporal and spatial scattering is applied. Fragments are spread randomly on various sites in a way that several fragments are not on the same location. This operation increases confidentiality because a number of concerted intrusions are necessary in order to gather all fragments. To recover a file in the FRS model a localization server is necessary.

In order to propose a decentralized architecture, we use flocking rules to avoid the use of centralized server, responsible of fragments localization. The aim is to allow the localization of all fragments by finding only one. So, the fragments position in the network is still unknown, but a cohesion between fragments is kept. These properties should allow to improve file request performance while keeping confidentiality.

To apply flocking rules in our model, we need a metric to measure distance between peers. We use a bitwise exclusive or (XOR) metric as in Kademlia [18].

Notation 2. *Let x,y be two peers identifiers. The distance d between them is given by* $: d(x,y) = x \oplus y.$

This metric have interesting properties:

- $d(x,x) = 0$,
- $d(x,y) > 0$ if $x \neq y$,
- $\forall x,y : d(x,y) = d(y,x)$
- $\forall x, \forall \Delta > 0$, there is one and only one y, such that $d(x,y) = \Delta$.

To choose peers where data fragments can move, we have to respect the following criteria :

- A given peer can store only one agent for a given document (separation rule).
- The agents move on peers in order to get closer to the most remote agent of the flock (cohesion rules using metric distance).
- The agents move on peers having less activity (the pheromones observation provides load balancing).
- The agents move on peers having a high trust level.

Algorithm 2. Flocking principle apply to fragment stored by a peer x

---

Input: A peer x, d a document, f_d a fragment of d
Output: A peer where store f_d
$busyPeers \leftarrow$ neighbors of x storing fragments $\in d$;
foreach $y \in busyPeers$ **do**
   if $d(x,y) < \lambda$ **then**
     | Remove $y \in busyPeers$ (violation of cohesion rule);

$freePeers \leftarrow$ neighbors of x with fragments $\notin d$;
foreach $y \in busyPeers$ and $z \in freePeers$ **do**
   if $d(y,z) > \lambda$ **then**
     | Remove $z \in freePeers$ (violation of cohesion rule);

Choose a peer $p \in freePeers$ with the higher trust level and the lower pheromone level;

These rules, applied to agents, allow to keep cohesion and a permanent mobility. It will be difficult for an intruder to guess where the fragments are stored.

In algorithm 2, we have to choose between multiple choice taking into account multiple criteria (pheromones and trust). This is a multi-criteria decision making (MCDM) problem ([19,20]). In such a problem, the max operator can't be apply.

$$\max_{MCDM} \{(\phi_1, \tau_1); (\phi_2, \tau_2); (\phi_3, \tau_3)\}$$

where ϕ_i is the pheromone level to a peer i, and τ_i the associated trust. This example shows some of the difficulties of MCDM. In our model, the pheromones level and the trust have been normalized, and a classical operator has been used:

– **Utilitarian Operators (i.e. Weighted Sum)**

$$\max_{MCDM} = \max_i(\alpha_\phi \phi_i + \alpha_\tau \tau_i),$$

where α_ϕ, α_τ are the weight of the criteria.

The weights define the agent preference between trust and local network load (pheromone level).

5   Experiments

We experimented our model with oRis [21], a multi-agent system simulator. We build a 400 peers network where each peer have a neighborhood of 24 peers. Experiments consist in evaluating load balancing, trust, and flock reaction to suspicious peers. In our simulations, a single document is fragmented in 20 agents, and then scattered. To evaluate robustness, we have made experiments with a network composed of 10% of suspicious nodes. A suspicious node is a peer decreasing his pheromone level faster than the others, in order to attract fragments. They are enabled after the 5000th simulation cycle.

Figure 6a depicts load balancing in the network. All the peers have been visited by the flock with a network composed of regular peers (black curve). All network capabilities have been used and the load have been balanced between all members. Comportment with suspicious nodes is described with the doted curve. Only 85% of our network have been visited. It shows that only regular peers have been used. This is confirmed by the figure 6b and the figure 6c.

The figure 6b describes the evolution of the pheromone level during time. A peak indicates a passage of the flock and the decrease is due to the pheromone evaporation. Peers have been visited several times during simulation (black curve). After the 5000th simulation cycle, a suspicious peer decrease his pheromone level faster than a regular peer (doted curve). Once the minimal level is reached, the pheromone level does not raise. This indicates that agents have not been stored on suspicious peers. Consequence of this rough fall is a decrease of the trust associated to these peers (doted curve in figure 6c). Therefore suspicious nodes are avoided by the flock.

The trust level in the network is depicted by the figure 6c. The maximum level is reached (100%) for a network composed of regular peers after 5000 simulation cycles (black curve). When suspicious nodes are actives (doted curve), they are detected by the others, and so their trust decrease.

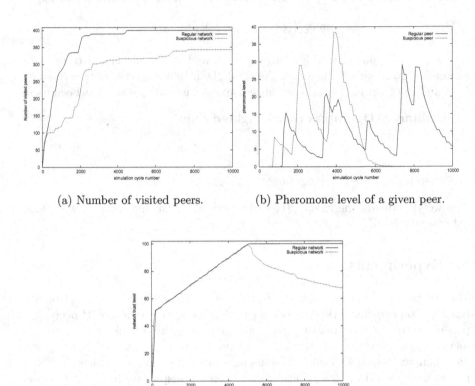

(a) Number of visited peers.   (b) Pheromone level of a given peer.

(c) Trust level in the network.

Fig. 6. Number of visited peers, pheromone level, and trust level during time

6 Discussion

Document retrieval is a problematic and many solutions are possible. We could introduce identified pheromones associated to a flock. So, a research agent follow the pheromones of a specific document. However this mechanism has obvious security drawbacks. The choice of our logical network layer can also influence the document search. Gossip-based overlay networks, are very interesting [22]. Such overlays are robust, and propose an efficient routing of information. A research agent could use this property to locate the flock and identify it.

In this paper, the global performance was not approached. Here clearly mobility have a cost, but the safety engendered by the load balancing is important.

But keeping a permanent network traffic allows not to deduce areas where fragments are located. So, to plan attacks on targeted peers, become very difficult.

Applications of a such platform, are also interesting. Here we presented a model of a P2P data storage application. Another application possible is a P2P mail service. Mails are the best example for sensitive data. Sending a mail, trigger a flock in the network. The receiver may retrieve the mail by steering the flock, and merging the fragments.

7 Conclusion

This paper presents a new model of a robust decentralized P2P architecture for data storage. This robustness is reached by using fragmentation, redundancy and fragments mobility. We use mobile agents to move fragments across the network. To manage agents moves, flocking rules are applied. So our agents form a flock, making easier the document retrieval. A trust establishment scheme, based on environment observation (pheromones), have been proposed. Another issue of using pheromones is the load balancing. Our flock try to move in areas having the less activity.

Our algorithms have been tested on simulations, and results are promising. Thanks to flocking rules and pheromones, a detection scheme of suspicious nodes is possible. An emergent property of the flock is the avoidance of these peers. Load balancing is also provided by our algorithms.

In a near future, we will test our model in a P2P simulator like Peersim. The relationship between security and performance will be studied. An implementation with JXTA or JADE can also be envisaged. We will also work on a secure and efficient search protocol in order to steer the flock in a peer where a request was made.

References

1. Rowstron, A., Druschel, P.: Storage management and caching in PAST, a large-scale, persistent peer-to-peer storage utility. In: Proc. of the 18th ACM Symposium on Operating System Principles (2001)
2. Rowstron, A., Druschel, P.: Pastry: Scalable, Decentralized Object Location, and Routing for Large-Scale Peer-to-Peer Systems. In: Guerraoui, R. (ed.) Middleware 2001. LNCS, vol. 2218, pp. 329–350. Springer, Heidelberg (2001)
3. Druschel, P., Rowstron, A.: PAST: A large-scale, persistent peer-to-peer storage utility. In: HotOS VIII, Schloss Elmau, Germany, pp. 75–80 (2001)
4. Rhea, S., Eaton, P., Geels, D., Weatherspoon, H., Zhao, B., Kubiatowicz, J.: Pond: The oceanstore prototype. In: Proceedings of the Conference on File and Storage Technologies. USENIX (2003)
5. Kubiatowicz, J., Bindel, D., Chen, Y., Eaton, P., Geels, D., Gummadi, R., Rhea, S., Weatherspoon, H., Weimer, W., Wells, C., Zhao, B.: Oceanstore: An architecture for global-scale persistent storage. In: Proceedings of ACM ASPLOS. ACM (2000)
6. Blomer, J., Kalfane, M., Karp, R., Karpinski, M., Luby, M., Zuckerman, D.: An xor-based erasure-resilient coding scheme. Technical report, International Computer Science Institute, Berkeley, California (1995)

7. Zhao, B., Kubiatowicz, J., Joseph, A.D.: Tapestry: An infrastructure for fault-tolerant wide-area location and routing. Technical Report UCB/CSD-01-1141, UC Berkeley (2001)
8. Clarke, I., Sandberg, O., Wiley, B., Hong, T.W.: Freenet: A Distributed Anonymous Information Storage and Retrieval System. In: Federrath, H. (ed.) Anonymity 2000. LNCS, vol. 2009, pp. 46–66. Springer, Heidelberg (2001)
9. Babaoglu, O., Meling, H., Montresor, A.: Anthill: A framework for the development of agent-based peer-to-peer systems. In: The 22th Int. Conf. on Distributed Computing Systems, Vienna, Austria (2002)
10. Deswarte, Y., Blain, L., Fabre, J.C.: Intrusion tolerance in distributed computing systems. In: IEEE Symposium on Security and Privacy, pp. 110–121 (1991)
11. Fabre, J.C., Deswarte, Y., Randell, B.: Designing Secure and Reliable Applications using Fragmentation-Redundancy-Scattering: An Object-Oriented Approach. In: Echtle, K., Powell, D.R., Hammer, D. (eds.) EDCC 1994. LNCS, vol. 852, pp. 21–38. Springer, Heidelberg (1994)
12. Reynolds, C.W.: Flocks, herds and schools: A distributed behavioral model. In: SIGGRAPH 1987: Proceedings of the 14th Annual Conference on Computer Graphics and Interactive Techniques, pp. 25–34. ACM, New York (1987)
13. Lindhé, M., Ögren, P., Johansson, K.H.: Flocking with obstacle avoidance: A new distributed coordination algorithm based on voronoi partitions. In: ICRA, pp. 1785–1790 (2005)
14. Gervasi, V., Prencipe, G.: Coordination without communication: the case of the flocking problem. Discrete Applied Mathematics 144, 324–344 (2004)
15. Wagner, L.: Byzantine agreements in secure communication. In: 5th Operations Research Conference on Secure Communication, ASOR (2003)
16. Lamport, L., Shostak, R.E., Pease, M.C.: The byzantine generals problem. ACM Trans. Program. Lang. Syst. 4, 382–401 (1982)
17. Shamir, A.: How to share a secret. Commun. ACM 22, 612–613 (1979)
18. Maymounkov, P., Mazières, D.: Kademlia: A Peer-to-Peer Information System Based on the XOR Metric. In: Druschel, P., Kaashoek, M.F., Rowstron, A. (eds.) IPTPS 2002. LNCS, vol. 2429, pp. 53–65. Springer, Heidelberg (2002)
19. Keeney, R.L., Raiffa, H.: Decisions with multiple objectives: Preferences and value tradeoffs. J. Wiley, New York (1976)
20. Galand, L., Perny, P.: Search for compromise solutions in multiobjective state space graphs. In: ECAI, pp. 93–97 (2006)
21. Harrouet, F., Tisseau, J., Reignier, P., Chevaillier, P.: oris: un environnement de simulation interactive multi-agents. Technique et Science Informatiques 21, 499–524 (2002)
22. Jelasity, M., Babaoglu, O.: T-Man: Gossip-Based Overlay Topology Management. In: Brueckner, S.A., Di Marzo Serugendo, G., Hales, D., Zambonelli, F. (eds.) ESOA 2005. LNCS (LNAI), vol. 3910, pp. 1–15. Springer, Heidelberg (2006)

Trustworthy Agent-Based Recommender System in a Mobile P2P Environment

Nabil Sahli[1], Gabriele Lenzini[2], and Henk Eertink[2]

[1] Dhofar University, Salalah, Sultanate of Oman
[2] Novay, P.O. Box 589, 7500 AN Enschede, The Netherlands
{gabriele.lenzini,henk.eertink}@novay.nl

Abstract. Current major P2P systems focus on PCs and do not provide services for the mobile environment. Compared to traditional P2P, characteristics of Mobile P2P include unreliable connections, limited bandwidth and constraints of mobile devices. In addition, nomadic users demand applications and services that are context-aware, personalised, secure, and trustworthy. Recommender systems are one of these applications. In this paper, we aim at building a mobile P2P recommender system which dramatically reduces wireless traffic between peers, brings trustworthiness (each peer can choose to rely on opinions of peers whom he trusts), and ffers unobtrusiveness (the target system is mainly autonomous and requires a minimum user intervention). Our solution is based on multi-agent systems and is illustrated on a slow-food restaurant recommender system.

1 Introduction

There is no doubt that mobile computing is increasingly important especially after the explosion of smartphones (networked PDA). While many distributed applications and services (e.g., file sharing) are still not appropriate for mobile devices because they require large hardware capabilities, others are more suitable. For instance, sharing opinions (e.g., recommendations) is an application which does not need a lot of resources (storage) and thus is a more appropriate mobile service. A mobile recommender system would certainly have many advantages over those which already exist on PC. Indeed, besides the ubiquitous access (members have an anytime-anyplace connection) advantage, the service can also be location based. For example, a mobile recommender system for restaurants would suggest good restaurants according to the current location of the user. The user could also rate a restaurant by geotagging[1], which frees him from entering the location information about the restaurant. Most successful recommender systems implemented so far are based on a client/server architecture where there is one central service provider and many users. In this architecture, the system collects the users' ratings (or opinions) and then applies an algorithm on the stored data to derive recommendations. However, when the trustworthiness

---

[1] *"The process of adding geographical identification metadata to media"* (Wikipedia).

D. Beneventano et al. (Eds.): AP2PC 2008/2009, LNAI 6573, pp. 59–70, 2012.

and the personalisation of these recommendations is an issue of great concern, a decentralised approach might be more appropriate. Unlike a centralised recommender (based on collaborative filtering) which relies on all peers' ratings, we suggest a decentralised recommender system which also considers ratings of peers on which a given user trusts.

Compared to traditional server/client technology on the Internet, the peer-to-peer (P2P) technology has capabilities to realise highly scalable, extensible and efficient decentralised recommender systems. However, current major P2P systems such as Gnutella and Napster, focus on PCs and do not provide services for the mobile environment. In fact, compared to traditional P2P, characteristics of Mobile P2P (MP2P) include unreliable connection, limited bandwidth and constraints of mobile devices (smaller screen, limited interface capabilities, restricted computational power). In addition, nomadic users demand applications and services that are context-aware, personalised, secure, and trustworthy. Most of current MP2P architectures are still suggesting a direct wireless communication between peers, which is demanding in terms of bandwidth and then communication reliability and cost.

The main idea of our work is to assign two agents to each mobile user: an *Embedded-Agent* which resides in the mobile device and captures the user's context and ratings, and a *Delegate-Agent* which resides in an open multi-agents architecture where it meets other peers. Using the context, the profile, and the experience (transmitted by the *Embedded-Agent*) of the user, *Delegate-Agent* maintains a personal community of trustworthy recommenders and a list of rated items. Consequently, we ensure more unobtrusiveness, trustworthiness, and context-awareness. Since all *Delegate-Agents* interact in a meeting space, wireless traffic between peers is dramatically reduced.

The rest of the paper is organised as follows. Section 2 presents a brief background on recommender systems (centralised vs. decentralised and content-based vs. collaborative filtering approaches). Section 3 describes our proposed architecture and its fundamental concepts. Section 4 is dedicated to the scenario we have implemented to recommend slow-food restaurants to a mobile community. Section 5 compares our approach to related works. Finally, Section 6 summarises our contributions and presents our future works.

2   Background on Recommender Systems

Two common ways of determining trust among peers are through using policies or reputation. Policies frequently involve the exchange or verification of *credentials*, which are information issued by one peer, and may describe qualities or features of another peer. Reputation (addressed here) is an assessment of a peer based on the history of interactions or observations, either directly (personal experience) or as reported by others (recommendations or third party verification). Various reputation-based systems have been proposed in different P2P systems. Two main approaches are used: centralised or decentralised.

In a centralised approach, observations about peers are reported and then stored in a central database. The reputation system (usually the central database itself) uses these data to calculate the reputation of each peer. This approach is used in the reputation systems of eBay and Amazon. This centralised approach is not compatible with the design philosophy of P2P systems. We thus address a decentralised approach which can offer the three following desirable features: (i) no central authority (individuals are not dependent on a global rating system), (ii) personalised reputation, which means that the reputation of a particular peer is not built upon the opinions of the whole community but rather of a group of selected peers, and (iii) peers' preferences and profiles are taken into account.

There has been research about moving recommender systems toward a distributed architecture while using agents (cf. [1–7]). In a decentralised approach, members store their own observations locally. If A wants to find out about the reputation of B, it looks for other peers that interacted with B (called witnesses) and asks them for their observations about B. In this approach, reputation is calculated in a distributed manner, which provides a level of freedom to peers in choosing the method of calculating reputation according to their beliefs and preferences. Besides and since each peer can choose its own witnesses, it provides him more confidence on the resulting reputation value compared to the centralised approach. Consequently, the decentralised approach is more convenient for open communities such as P2P systems.Our work is related to these aforementioned systems. Differences are discussed in Section 5.

3   Proposed Approach

In this section, we briefly introduce the main concepts which are used in our approach: the Virtual Agora, the Register of (Un)Trusted Recommender and the Register of Trusted Items.

Virtual Agora (VA). It is a virtual open space (e.g. web site, server) where peers meet, interact, share experiences about items of interest. Items are advertised in the VA (i.e., only their names and characteristics are known within the VA). For instance an item can represent a restaurant and its description. The VA concept suggests three main characteristics: (i) Openness which means that peers from various sources can freely join or leave the VA at any time, (ii) no central authority that controls peers, and (iii) persistence of these peers (if desired) within the VA, which also suggests the persistence of the VA and its continuous availability.

Register of (Un)Trusted Recommender (TRec). From the subjective viewpoint of a peer A, TRec is the set of peers (met in the VA) whose (positive or negative) trustworthiness has been evaluated by A. A will consult them when she/he needs an opinion about a certain item. The term "subjective" means that each peer has a personalised TRec. For example, let us suppose that peer A is interested in Bikes. It joins a VA whose members are interested in the subject "bikes". A mets {B;C;D;E;F;G;L;..} and after some interactions forms her initial TRec (see [8] for more details) composed of {B;C;D;E} as illustrated in Fig. 1. B, instead, may have a different community (e.g., {A;C;F;G;L}). From this point of view, our TRec concept is similar to wide-spread communities such as Msn Messenger (http://www.messenger.com) but as we will see, the trustworthiness of each is explicitly maintained.

Register of Trusted Items (TRat). It describes how much a peer trusts a set of items. Each relationship is weighted with the current rating that A gives to the item. The ratings are subjective to the member's profile and way of judging. We assume that the members of the community share some algebra of rating. Moreover, aside to the rating itself, the relationship keeps log of the information used to compose the rating (i.e. recommendations and recommenders). For example, in Fig. 1 b., *item2* is rated 3 by C (following a direct experience, i.e. C is the rater) and 4 by B (here B is not the initial rater but it is rather L).

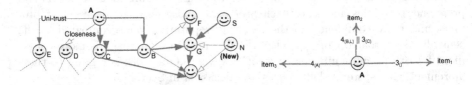

Fig. 1. a) Trusted Recommender and b) Trusted Ratings concepts

Both TRec and TRat have the following characteristics: (i) trust-based: the respective elements are linked by trust relationships, (ii) dynamic: trust relationships are continuously updated, and (iii) self-organised: members autonomously organise their trust relationships.

3.1 General Architecture

An appropriate architecture for a system which will support our approach should fulfill the requirements mentioned in Section 1. To this end, we propose the architecture illustrated in Fig. 2. The idea is to assign two agents to each mobile user. One agent (*Embedded-Agent*) is embedded in the mobile device and one agent (*Delegate-Agent*) is representing the mobile user in the VA. We thus decouple the "classical" *peer* into two pieces. In what follows we describe the main components of the architecture and demonstrate how the requirements mentioned above are achieved.

Virtual Agora. It is a meeting place for peers' *Delegate-Agents*. It includes a *Bulletin Board* and a *Policy Manager*. The former is required while the latter (gray in the Figure) is optional (depending on the application).

Bulletin Board. It is in charge of searching peers. In P2P networks, searching can be centralised (e.g. Napster has a resource directory server), distributed (in pure P2P networks like Gnutella), or intermediate (e.g. KaZaA) based

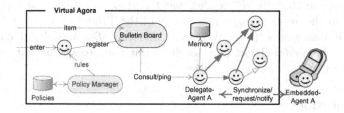

Fig. 2. Simplified Global Architecture (rounded rectangles refer to components)

on *nodes* and *supernodes*. In our architecture we opt for a centralised solution, named Bulletin Board (BB). This component is part of the VA and is managing the list of agents within the VA. A new agent in the VA can consult this list to discover other similar peers. Later, the agent relies more on its own network of peers (TRec), which considerably frees the BB. To keep its list up-to-date, the BB has to register new agents joining the agora and periodically ping agents in its list in order to check their availability. Moreover, BB keeps the list of items to be evaluated. We suppose that each item is uniquely identified among all peers.

Policy Manager. It is optional and used to grant rights and dictate rules and policies to different types of agents if the application requires such features. In this paper we do not focus on this component.

Delegate-Agent. This agent is hosted in the VA to represent the user vis-a-vis other peers. By interacting with other peers, it builds the TRec/TRat of its end-user and answers requests of recommendations (coming from its user or other peers). It is thus aware of its user's profile and preferences.

Embedded-Agent. This light agent (i.e. has few data and functionalities) is a proxy between the user and the *Delegate-Agent*. It mainly (i) notifies *Delegate-Agent* about user's ratings and tags, changes of interests or preferences, (ii) sends the updated user context to *Delegate-Agent*, and (iii) requests recommendations on behalf of the user.

Memory. Each *Delegate-Agent* has its own memory where it stores data which are useful when building the TRec/TRat or interacting with pairs.

Let us show how this architecture can fulfill the requirements presented in the introduction. By using the *Delegate* and *Embedded* agents, we allow mobile users to take advantage of the VA concept (to meet other peers). Besides, since a minimum interaction (to synchronise their data, to send and receive requests, and to notify each other about important changes) is needed between the two agents, the use of the wireless network is dramatically reduced. All interactions between the *Delegate-Agent* and the members of its TRec are indeed executed locally (in the VA). Regarding, managing the registration and discovery of the VA's members is ensured by the *BB* (and potentially by the *Policy Manager*).

Our VA-based solution is not a pure decentralised approach and therefore it may have a single point of failure (if the VA becomes temporarily unavailable).

We thus propose that the *Embedded-Agent* periodically (e.g., daily or weekly depending on the application) sends a copy of the TRat to the *Delegate-Agent*. If the VA is unavailable (for any reason) and that *Delegate-Agent* cannot be reached, the *Embedded-Agent* may use its TRat copy (certainly not optimised but still useful) to advice the end-user.

3.2   Agent Models

The *Belief-Desire-Intension* (BDI) model [9] has evolved over time and has been applied in several of the most significant multiagent applications developed up to now. It actually offers an interesting framework to design deliberative agents which are able to act and interact autonomously and according to their mental states. This model is the most appropriate for Delegate-Agents. We propose a BDI-based architecture which main components are illustrated in Fig. 3.

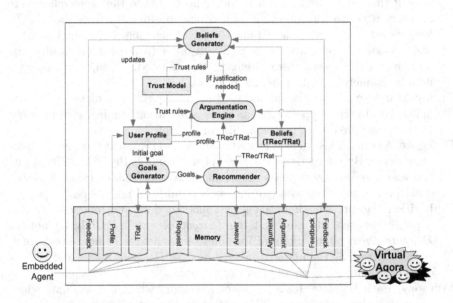

Fig. 3. Functional view of the Delegate Agent's BDI architecture

In what follows we describe the processes (rounded rectangles) and how they are related to the different data (rectangles). In the "Memory" component, two different shapes are used to show whether the data is an input (e.g. *Profile*) or an output (e.g. *Answer*).

– **Goals Generator.** It generates the goal(s) that the agent has to follow. When it first joins the VA, an initial goal is to build a TRec/TRat according to its user's profile. Later, its goals are dictated by specific requests coming from its user or members of the VA. This component generates then goals (which match the *Desire* concept in the BDI model) for the *Recommender*.

- **Beliefs Generator.** It generates the agent's beliefs received from the user (as feedback sent by the *Embedded-Agent*) or from other agents (as feedback or argument). While the former type of information is directly added as a belief, the latter is filtered according to a *trust model* and an *argumentation* process if necessary (see below). Final beliefs represent what the agent trusts and this corresponds to *Beliefs* in the BDI model.
- **Argumentation Engine.** This process is in charge of arguing with other agents in order to help the *Beliefs Generator* building its beliefs. For example, when the agent receives conflicting recommendations from different "trustful" peers, it can ask them to justify their opinions and argues with them in order to make a better choice regarding these recommendations. We describe the argumentation model in [10].
- **Recommender.** It uses the generated beliefs in order to answer incoming requests (from *Embedded* or other peers of the VA). The *Argumentation Engine* and the *Recommender* correspond to the BDI's *Intensions*.
- **Memory.** All inputs and outputs are stored in the *Memory* (see Fig. 3). Depending on the end-user's preference and the type of application, certain data are stored as long-term memory while others as short-term memory.
- **Beliefs.** Following Castelfranchi's postulate "Believe only if you have reasons to believe" [11], we make a distinction between memory and knowledge, between storing an information and accepting/believing it. Data stored in *Memory* are thus filtered to obtain *Beliefs* (represented by the TRec/TRat).
- **User's Profile.** It is composed of the user's *Preferences, Expertise,* and *Context.* The *Preferences* can be used for instance to discover how the user prefers the agent to present the information to him. *Expertise* is the skill or knowledge of a person who knows a great deal about a specific thing. Another important piece of information considered in the user's profile is the *Context* (location, time, social context, etc., see Section 6).
- **Trust Model.** This is the set of trust-based rules that the agent has to follow to infer trustworthy relationships (see Sub-section 3.3 and [8]).

While *Delegate-Agent* is deliberative, *Embedded-Agent* is more a reactive agent [12]. Indeed, the latter does not support any reasoning, it is only making the bridge between the user and the *Delegate-Agent*. It thus mainly reacts to incoming events. The main components of this reactive architecture are:

- **Interface.** This component interfaces with the user to get his requests or profile data and answer his requests.
- **Synchroniser.** It is in charge of synchronising data with *Delegate-Agent*. It mainly sends it requests and receives its answers, notifies it about changes on the user's profile, periodically requests a copy of the TRat, and forwards user's feedback to it.
- **Beliefs.** The *Embedded-Agent* only needs a copy of the TRat to be used in case of a VA failure. This is thus the only content of the *Beliefs*.
- **User's Profile.** Same as for the *Delegate-Agent*. Indeed, it is the *Embedded-Agent* which sends this profile to its *Delegate-Agent*.

3.3   Trust Evolution in TRec/TRat

According to to the literature, agent A's trust in item i is built from direct experiences [7] or from indirect experiences [4] (coming from other peers) or from a combination of both. Instead of using an unknown network of recommenders, we propose that A uses its own TRec to obtain focused recommendations (represented by TRat) about i. After being initialised, TRat and TRec are continuously updated and consulted. Due to the space constraint, we only present the general idea of these phases and do not talk about other important parameters for trust evaluation such as *Time* and *Context*. Our formal model of trust is described in [8] while solutions to integrate *Context* and to calculate similarities can be found in [13].

Bootstrapping. If A is new in the VA, it first has to build its initial TRec. To this end, it forms *Agent Closeness* (a weak trust relationship) relationships (Fig. 1 a.) with agents showing similar profiles and preferences as its user. If no agent similarities are found, it may establish *Closeness* relationships with few agents which are judged by the VA as trustful (these are agents who are the most trusted by other peers, i.e. present in many peers' TRecs). A has also to build its initial TRat by adding items that are potentially interesting for this user (for example in Fig. 1 b., A rates *item1* 3 using *item closeness*), or by asking members (recommenders) of its TRec (for example in Fig. 1 b., A receives two ratings about *item2*: 4 from B and 3 from C). These recommendations are not necessarily the result of the recommenders' direct experience (e.g., in Fig. 1 b., while C recommends *item2* using its direct experiences, B suggests a recommendation (4) of one of its TRec's members, L).

Consulting. When its end-user (or another peer of its TRec) requests a recommendation, A consults its TRat to reply to the request. If the information is not available in its TRat, it directly asks (by sending messages) its trustful recommenders (those in its TRec). When A has several recommendations about i, it weights them according to the trust relationships it has with these recommenders. For example, in Fig. 1 a. and from the perspective of A, a recommendation coming from E (*closeness*) has more weight that one coming from D (*uni-trust*, which reflects trust after direct experience).

Updating. Even if the end-user is not requesting any recommendations, A continually remains in the VA and whenever it receives a new information from another trusted peer, it updates its TRat (and eventually TRec if a new *close* peer has joined the VA) consequently. When A now receives a feedback from its user (following a direct experience) about i, it does not only update TRat, but also adjusts its trust relationships with its TRec's members based on what they had previously suggested about i. For example, if B turns out to be good recommender, A changes its trust relationship on B from *closeness* to *uni-trust*.

4   Implemented Scenario

Let us suppose that Bob is interested in slow-food. He wants to (i) find good slow-food restaurants in his city (or cities he is visiting), (ii) asks for reliable recommendations about specific restaurants from people having the same preferences as him, and (iii) share his own experience with other fans of slow-food. He signs up in a slow-food Virtual Agora (interfaced by a Web site to facilitate access for users) and sends a *Delegate-Agent* (called MyDelegate) to this Agora. Regarding the Embedded-Agent (EA-Bob), it has already been installed in Bob's mobile phone. In this scenario we do not use argumentation (see Sub-section 3.2) since the mechanism is not implemented yet.

By signing up, Bob has to fill in a form about his preferences concerning slow-food restaurants. For instance, he has to indicate which criteria are the most important according to him to rate a restaurant (price, quality of food, or service, etc.) or how he rates certain specific restaurants (in Fig. 4, he has one personal rating about restaurant R3). This information would be used by MyDelegate to argue when conflicting ratings arise (during the argumentation process) but mainly to build its initial TRec/TRat. Let us suppose that 3 agents (among others) Member1, Member2, and Member4 are now part of the TRec of MyDelegate and that MyDelegate has a *Closeness* relationship with all of them (value of trust in each member is "1", see Fig. 4). While building its initial TRat, and given the description (in the *BB*) of restaurant R4, MyDelegate decides to collect recommendations about R4. It then asks its TRec's members for advice and receives two conflicting recommendations about R4: Member4 recommends the restaurant (value="5", see Fig. 4) while Member1 and Member2 do not (value="1"). MyDelegate adds these different ratings to its TRat (concerning item R4). We suppose now that Bob is intending to have diner in restaurant R4 and that in the meaning while TRat has remained unchanged (i.e., MyDelegate did not receive any new information about R4 from its recommenders). Bob interacts then with his mobile to ask for recommendation. EA-Bob forwards the request to MyDelegate. This latter, noticing that R4 is in its TRat, tries to derive a personal rating about R4. Since Member4 is not more trustworthy than the two others, and without an argumentation mechanism (in this case), MyDelegate process an average rating (here $7/3=2.33$) and communicates the chosen rating (2.33 over 5) to EA-Bob. Given the low rating, Bob decides not to go to the restaurant.

Let us suppose now that, few days later, Bob was invited in R4 restaurant by his friend and that contrarily to his expectations he appreciated his meal. He thus used his mobile to positively rate the restaurant before he left.

EA-Bob forwards this rating (for example "4.5" to MyDelegate which uses Bob's feedback to assess its TRec/TRat. In this case, the feedback confirms that Member4 was right and is likely to be trustful whereas Member1 and Member2 are maybe not. As a consequence, MyDelegate strengthens its relationship with Member4 by giving a higher weight to the corresponding link that becomes a *Uni-trust* and weakens its relationship with Member1 and Member2 by giving a lower weight to the corresponding *closeness* links. MyDelegate also update the

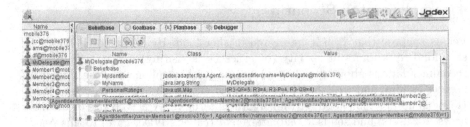

Fig. 4. Snapshot of the MyDelegate Agent in Jadex environment (due to the space constraint, we highlight data with tooltips)

TRat by assigning "4.5" (as a direct experience of Bob) to R4. An argumentation mechanism would have allowed MyDelegate to make a better choice about R4 since MyDelegate could have had justifications about these contradictory recommendations and could have decided according to Bob's profile and to how much arguments and proofs (of recommenders) are strong and acceptable.

We chose Jadex [14] as a development environment for the VA. Besides the fact that Jadex extends a reliable environment (Jade), it handles the BDI concept which is very useful in our case to easier implement the VA's members. We are currently working on integrating context and argumentation aspects.

5   Related Work

Most of the decentralised agent-based recommender systems [1–7] present four main differences with our approach. First, and except [6], they are all not suitable for mobile environments (require huge traffic between remote peers). Second, most of them use witness reputation mechanisms (e.g. [4, 5, 7]). In our approach we only use members' reputation in the bootstrapping phase, if the agent has no past relevant experience. Our list of trusted pairs is rather more subjective (first built according to closeness and then updated based on direct experience). Third, to our knowledge, none of the existing systems (including [6]) has proposed a decentralised recommender system which supports a high level of personalisation. In fact, a peer gets a much smaller set of opinions (in number) when asking for a recommendation. Nevertheless, these opinions are of high quality since they are more personalised (trusted source, justified opinions, similar context and profile). We actually focus on quality (of recommendations) rather than on quantity. Finally, in most of the existing distributed recommender systems, when a peer leaves the community the referral pointers become obsolete and the knowledge of the quitter is lost. In our system and since each peer shares its knowledge with the community, we claim that a peer's knowledge will remain available within peers which have accepted it (after argumentation). We thus enhance the persistence of knowledge in P2P systems.

With respect to the proposed architecture (Fig. 2), similar concepts to VA can be found in the literature. For example, the *Advertisement Infrastructure* [15] is a space where agents can build collaborative plans, while the ToothAgent system [16] offers a centralised service that agents use to interact and to meet servers on behalf of their users. The VA novelty is to allow entities to build their own subjective network of trust (TRec and TRat). Recommendation are not processed equally for all the members and items are not rated independently form the tastes of a subject or his/her past experiences.

6 Conclusion and Future Work

In this paper we presented an agent-based architecture for mobile P2P recommending systems. By decoupling a peer into two agents (*Delegate* and *Embedded*), our approach allows to dramatically reduce wireless traffic between peers (a mobile peer has a limited interaction with its representative in the VA). By adopting a BDI model, we also give agents more autonomy, which considerably frees users from managing their trust on other peers. From the recommender system perspective, it also goes beyond the traditional collaborative filtering approach by allowing each peer (a BDI agent) to manage its own trust on other peers, which ensures more reliable and trustworthy recommendations. By doing so, we go a step further than similar works such as [6] or TAKEUP [17].

As future work, we intend to integrate our argumentation model [10] in the prototype, which will allow peers to make better choices when evaluating recommendations. Besides, and given that the current prototype has only focus on the *Delegate-Agent* side (and the Virtual Agora), we are also working on the *Embedded-Agent* side and especially on integrating the context to our architecture. One way of capturing context is via *ContextWatcher* [18]; it is a mobile application developed in our research lab, and which aims at making it easy for an end-user to automatically record, store, and use context information. This context information will be used as an input parameter for the *Embedded-Agent* and forwarded to the *Delegate-Agent*. This later will use this information to evaluate its trust on received recommendations. For instance, let us suppose that each user's tagging (or rating) of a certain restaurant R4 will be associated with the context captured by ContextWatcher (e.g., time and location). A *Delegate-Agent* would then probably trust a rating which was recently made in the same city as R4 more than an out-dated rating which was made far from the R4's neighborhood. The *Delegate-Agent* can also use this contextual data during the argumentation process in order to evaluate proofs.

References

1. Foner, L.: Yenta: A multi-agent, referral based matchmaking system. In: Proc. of the 1st Int. Conf. on Autonomous Agents, pp. 301–307. ACM (1997)
2. Miller, B., Konstan, J., Riedl, J.: Toward a personal recommender system. ACM Transactions on Information Systems 22, 437–476 (2004)

3. Olsson, T.: Bootstrapping and Decentralizing Recommender Systems. PhD thesis, Uppsala University and SICS (2006)

4. Sabater, J., Sierra, C.: Social regret, a reputation model based on social relations. SIGecom Exchanges 3, 44–56 (2002)

5. Teacy, W., Patel, J., Jennings, N., Luck, M.: Coping with inaccurate reputation sources: Experimental analysis of a probabilistic trust model. In: Proc. of the 4th Int. Joint Conf. AAMAS, pp. 997–1004 (2005)

6. Tveit, A.: Peer-to-peer based recommendations for mobile commerce. In: Proc. of the 1st Int. Workshop on Mobile Commerce (WMC 2001), pp. 26–29. ACM, Rome (2001)

7. Yu, B., Singh, M.P.: An evidential model of distributed reputation management. In: Proc. of 1st Int. Joint Conference on Autonomous Agents and Multi-Agent Systems, AAMAS 2002, Bologna, Italy, July 15-19, pp. 294–301 (2002)

8. Lenzini, G., Sahli, N., Eertink, H.: Agents Selecting Trustworthy Recommendations in Mobile Virtual Communities. In: Falcone, R., Barber, S.K., Sabater-Mir, J., Singh, M.P. (eds.) Trust 2008. LNCS (LNAI), vol. 5396, pp. 182–204. Springer, Heidelberg (2008)

9. Rao, A.S., Georgeff, M.: Bdi agents: from theory to practice. In: Proc. of the 1st Int. Conference on Multi-Agent Systems (ICMAS 1995), June 12-14, pp. 312–319. AAAI Press, San Francisco (1995)

10. Lenzini, G., Sahli, N.: Argumentation-based trust in recommender systems. In: Proc. of the Special session: Trust in Pervasive Systems and Networks, at SE-CRYPT part of the ICETE - The Int. Joint Conf. on e-Business and Telecommunications, Porto, Portugal (2008) (to appear)

11. Castelfranchi, C.: Reasons to believe: cognitive models of beliefs change. In: Proc. of the Int. Workshop on Cognitive, Computational and Logical Approaches to Belief Change, Amsterdam, The Netherlands (2004)

12. Brooks, R.A.: Intelligence without representation. Artificial Intelligence 47, 139–159 (1991)

13. Toivonen, S., Lenzini, G., Uusitalo, I.: Context-aware trustworthiness evaluation with indirect knowledge. In: Proc. of the 2nd Semantics Web Policy Workshop, ISWC 2006, Athens GA, USA. CEUR Workshop Proc. (2006), http://CEUR-WS.org

14. JADEX (2008), http://vsis-www.informatik.uni-hamburg.de/projects/jadex/

15. Maamar, Z., Sahli, N., Moulin, B., Labbe, P.: A software agent-based collaborative approach for humanitarian-assistance scenarios. Information and Security: An Int. Journal 8, 135–155 (2002)

16. Bryl, V., Giorgini, P., Fante, S.: ToothAgent: A Multi-agent System for Virtual Communities Support. In: Kolp, M., Henderson-Sellers, B., Mouratidis, H., Garcia, A., Ghose, A.K., Bresciani, P. (eds.) AOIS 2006. LNCS (LNAI), vol. 4898, pp. 212–230. Springer, Heidelberg (2008)

17. Schulz, S., Herrmann, K., Kalcklösch, R., Schwotzer, T.: TAKEUP: Trust-Based Agent-Mediated Knowledge Exchange for Ubiquitous Peer Networks. In: van Elst, L., Dignum, V., Abecker, A. (eds.) AMKM 2003. LNCS (LNAI), vol. 2926, pp. 89–106. Springer, Heidelberg (2004)

18. Koolwaaij, J., Tarlano, A., Luther, M., Nurmi, P., Mrohs, B., Battestini, A., Vaidya, R.: Contextwatcher - sharing context information in everyday life: In: Proc. of the IASTED International Conference on Web Technologies, Applications, and Services (WTAS 2006), pp. 39–60. ACTA Press, Calgary (2006)

Efficient Algorithms for Agent-Based Semantic Resource Discovery

António Luís Lopes and Luís Miguel Botelho

We, the Body, and the Mind Research Lab of Adetti-ISCTE,
Av. Forças Armadas, Edifício ISCTE, 1600-082 Lisboa, Portugal
{antonio.luis,luis.botelho}@iscte.pt
http://www.we-b-mind.org

Abstract. A semantic overlay network is a powerful mechanism for collaborative environments where multiple agents, managing several resources, can cooperate in pursuing common and individual goals while achieving good overall performance. However, building such a social structure dynamically from an unstructured peer-to-peer network is a lengthy process if appropriate algorithms and techniques are not used. In this paper, we analyse a set of network evolution techniques that improve the performance of classic approaches, such as the *flooding* search algorithm. We compare the efficiency of these enhanced classic algorithms with our previously proposed search algorithm, which has also been improved through the referred techniques. Evaluation tests show that the improved version of our algorithm outperforms the improved version of the classic search algorithm and efficiently creates a semantic overlay network for agent-based resource coordination.

Keywords: search algorithms, semantic overlay networks, peer-to-peer networks, intelligent agents.

1   Introduction

Research on peer-to-peer (*P2P*) computing has delivered promising results, paving the way for developing more robust and scalable applications. Nevertheless, these research efforts have mainly addressed the efficient management of the network, treating each peer as a simple reactive node, with little or no autonomy at all, thus ignoring the potential for developing collaborative environments. In our research, we envision the combination of the distributed capabilities of *P2P* networks with the intelligence of autonomous agents to deploy resource coordination systems allowing seamless access to large-scale distributed resources while maintaining high-availability, fault tolerance and low maintenance application deployment through self-organization.

A resource coordination system is an environment where agents, managing different resources, can cooperate to provide value-added services, which could not be provided if the agents were to operate individually. The heterogeneous and distributed environment of *P2P* networks offers the potential for building powerful applications based on resource coordination. A *semantic overlay network* [7] can enhance the resource sharing process in such distributed networks by establishing semantic links

D. Beneventano et al. (Eds.): AP2PC 2008/2009, LNAI 6573, pp. 71–82, 2012.

between agents based on similarities or dependencies between the resources that they manage. In our work, the semantic links are built based on the formal description of resources. For example, an executable resource (a web service or program) can be described through its inputs, outputs, pre-conditions (conditions that need to be true prior to the execution of the resource) and effects (conditions that are made true after the execution of the resource). If resource A's effects contribute to resource B's pre-conditions, then we say that B is *dependent* on A or that A *enables* B. Instead of blindly searching the network, semantically guided search processes direct the search to the agents that are more likely to own the required resources. Unfortunately, building a semantic overlay on top of a network of randomly-connected agents can be a very lengthy process if efficient algorithms are not used.

In previously published work [17], we have proposed the use of a dynamically created semantic overlay network as the basis upon which to build an efficient and effective self-improving agent-based resource coordination system. This included the proposal of a set of search algorithms and network evolution techniques to enhance the resource discovery process in which the agents interact to jointly build a semantic overlay network. This paper focuses on the evaluation of the proposed network evolution techniques by describing the results of applying them to a classic search algorithm (the *flooding* algorithm) and on the evaluation of one of the proposed algorithms, the *Iterative Branching Depth-First Search* (*IBDFS*) algorithm. In section 2, we present related work on search mechanisms and agent-based resource discovery mechanisms. Section 3 briefly describes the network evolution techniques that we have used to enhance classical approaches and the *IBDFS* algorithm and analyses the effects that each of those techniques has on the overall performance of the algorithms. The analysis done in section 3 allows us to conclude that a specific configuration of the *flooding* algorithm (*IF12*) is the best option to dynamically create a semantic overlay network. In section 4, we compare the performance of the enhanced classical algorithm (*IF12*) with the improved version of the *IBDFS* algorithm by analysing the results of several different tests, which show that our algorithm outperforms the *IF12* algorithm (both in result retrieval speed and network coverage) in all variations of the tests. Section 5 concludes the paper and provides some guidelines for future work.

2   Related Work

In distributed networks, where the goal is to build a collaborative environment to facilitate resource sharing, resources need to be easily located so that they can be aggregated and/or executed. Resource coordination research addresses these issues. One of the most important aspects of resource coordination is the discovery process, in which peers[1] perform search requests within the network to find the resources that they need to achieve their goals. A resource can be instantiated as a web service, a file, an intelligent agent capability, storage or processing capabilities or any other computational skill available in a network of interconnected peers.

---

[1] Since the agents on the referred resource coordination system are part of P2P networks (thus playing the role of peers), we sometimes refer to them as *peers*. We do not, however, wish to state that the terms *peer* and *agent* have the same meaning.

2.1   Search Algorithms

The nature of the search process in a resource discovery environment depends on the type of network where agents operate. In *unstructured* networks (where all peers are equal in responsibilities and no hierarchy exists) peers cannot rely on any information to optimize the search process. Searching a certain network resource or peer is often carried out by using *blind* algorithms (in the sense that agents randomly query other agents), such as *flooding* or *random walk* algorithms. Both algorithms present some disadvantages: *flooding* increases network load with copies of the query message but may retrieve the results faster, whereas the *random walk* reduces the network load but increases the search latency. In an effort to improve their performance, some search mechanisms based on variations of these two algorithms were created. *Iterative deepening* [27] is an example of an improved *flooding* search mechanism. It initiates multiple *breadth-first* searches, over the iterations of the technique, with successively larger depth limits, until either the query is satisfied, or a maximum depth limit has been reached. However, this only improves the network coverage of the *flooding* algorithm, not its ability for obtaining results faster.

An alternative to these *blind* search algorithms is on the use of *informed* algorithms. In this type of search, peers use additional information about other peers' resources (usually, obtained from previous queries) to select the ones that will be contacted during the search process [5]. For example, *Routing Indices* [6] allow peers to forward queries to a subset of neighbours (which is identified by evaluating an index table that contains the inventory of resources of the neighbouring peers [20]) that are the best candidates to satisfy the query. Similar approaches are exploited in the *Directed Breadth-First Search* [27] and in the *Intelligent Search* mechanism [13] where each peer in the network builds a profile (set of properties) of its peers and uses that profile to determine which ones are more likely to answer each query. Other informed search approaches, which use feedback from previous searches to improve future ones, include *Adaptive Probabilistic Searches* [26] and *Directed Searches* [18], which rely upon statistic information about other peers, including their performance. Unfortunately, these algorithms for unstructured networks use some form of the *Depth-First Search* or *Random Walk* search mechanisms that, even though are able to reduce the network traffic, increase the search latency, thus taking more time to return the queries results.

In *structured* networks, the existence of an organizational structure helps improving search performance by facilitating message routing between the peers. A network structure usually establishes some sort of hierarchy between the peers, such as partitioning the network into a set of communicating clusters of peers that are connected amongst them by a network of *super-peers*. However, hierarchical approaches such as the ones based on these special-purpose peers come at the expense of resilience to semi-catastrophic failures of *super-peers* near the top of the hierarchy [4]. A scalable and yet robust infrastructure for *P2P* networks relies on *Distributed Hash Tables* (*DHT*). *Chord* [25], *Pastry* [22], *Tapestry* [28] and *CAN* [19] are examples of DHT implementations. Although semantic-free approaches, such as *DHT*, provide good performance for point queries (where the search key is known exactly), they are not as effective for approximate, range, or text queries [7] and they do not, on their own, capture the relationships between the resource or peer's name and its content or metadata [21].

2.2   Agent-Based Resource Discovery

Early attempts for dealing with resource discovery issues [23] were based on the use of dedicated central servers. However, centralized solutions were deemed unsuitable for large environments and later approaches decided to use the hybrid potential of *P2P* networks, such as dynamic federated environments [24], where *super-peers* share their peers' resources by federating with other content-related *super-peers*; structured networks with resource rating [9]; and distributed multi-registry centres [16][12], where peers register their resources in the appropriate registry centres based on their type or the domain in which they operate. Unfortunately, using properties such as *type* and *domain* is not enough to represent complex connections between resources. An effective way to enhance resource coordination is to establish semantic connections between agents based on the properties of their resources, as these semantic links can be used to improve future searches and collaboration initiatives. The process of establishing meaningful connections in a network of randomly-connected agents may bring, however, some problems regarding efficiency and scalability, especially in large-scale systems.

Some systems rely on structured solutions, such as aggregation of peers [14] in communities [2] or the use of middle layers that have specific coordination capabilities [10][15]. Structured systems contribute to enhance the routing mechanisms in *P2P* computing, however, at the cost of introducing central points of failure such as special-purpose agents (like mediators) and hierarchical dependency relations. To avoid these failure-prone solutions, some approaches are based on pure *P2P* networks. An inference system based on pure *P2P* networks is presented in [1]. In this approach, each peer can answer queries by reasoning from its local (propositional) theory but can also perform queries to some other peers with which it is semantically related by sharing part of its knowledge. In order to create these semantic relations (referred by the authors as *acquaintance networks*), new peers joining the *P2P* system simply declare their *acquaintances* in the network, i.e., the peers they know to be sharing knowledge with, and they declare the corresponding shared variables. However, the authors do not clearly explain how the "*acquaintances declaration*" process is carried out efficiently in the *P2P* network.

The study of ant communities has inspired some research on the development of *P2P* systems based on multi-agent systems. *Anthill* [3] is a *P2P*-based *MAS* which emulates the resource coordination behaviour of ants. In this framework, storage or computational resources (referred to as "*nests*") generate requests (referred to as "*ants*") in response to user requests. These *ants* travel across the network of *nests* in order to be processed and executed. *Ants* do not communicate directly with each other. Instead, they communicate indirectly by leaving information related to the service they are implementing in the appropriate resource manager found in the visited *nests*. This *pheromone*-like approach, also called "*stigmergy*", allows the network to self-organize and improve its performance over time. The idea of assigning agents to carry on requests (*ants*) avoids a non-scalable flooding search technique, since each *ant* will only travel to a *nest* at a time and will not replicate itself. However, the search performance might not be the best (it is, in fact, equivalent to the *Depth-first Search* algorithm that presents a poor performance compared to other search mechanisms [17]) because each edge of the network (*nests*) is only travelled once at a time for each request. The selection of the next *nest* to be visited by an *ant* can either have a deterministic approach (once the network is organized and appropriate overlay networks are available) or a totally random (*uninformed*) approach. A similar approach to [3] is proposed in [8], where mobile agents use *pheromone*-like behaviour to optimize the trails within a *P2P* network. However, instead of using the update process based on the path where the query originally came (which, as shown in section 3, limits the performance of the search algorithm), as in [3], the mobile agent creates a referral to the query-answering node, thus creating a direct link that will improve future similar searches. Unfortunately, this too uses an equivalent search algorithm to the *Depth-first Search*, which has a poor performance.

3   Network Evolution Techniques

One of the main aspects of our research is the process of dynamically building a semantic overlay on top of a network of randomly connected agents. The semantic overlay network is built through a self-organization process in which the new agents (that are introduced into the network) broadcast, according to a specific protocol, the description of their resources and needs (resources that they depend on) to the remaining agents. This information exchange allows agents to find the resources that they need (and the agents that manage them) and building a set of meaningful connections that will be useful later on, in this collaborative environment. Such a mechanism can, nevertheless, overload the entire network with requests. Thus, it is very important to devise an algorithm that allows the network to self-organise without compromising its efficiency, scalability and robustness. Some of the approaches that we analysed (see section 2) use some interesting mechanisms to improve the performance of the network in the resource discovery process. However, none of the approaches combines all those mechanisms. We have combined these into a set of techniques (including one that is not used by any of the considered approaches) that, by making use of network evolution properties, can improve the performance of any search algorithm in the process of building a semantic overlay network.

3.1   Informed Searches, Direct Replies and Referrals

In the beginning of the search process, agents in a *P2P* network do not have enough information about other agents since they are randomly connected to each other. As they go along, the interactions between them become valuable sources of information that can be used to guide future searches. Furthermore, the use of informed search techniques scales a lot better throughout time as agents improve their connections with other agents based on previous interactions [11].

In order for an agent to improve its participation in future searches, it is important that it caches information from previous search processes, as it is done in [6] [13] [18] [26] and [27]. For example, as a query response travels back to the requester agent, all agents in that specific path can either store the response themselves (*Anthill* [3]) or cache a link to the agent which has the response, thus working as a referral for future searches (as in [8]). An alternative approach can be based on the query response being returned directly to the query requester, instead of being carried back through the path originally travelled by the query. For example, if agent *A1* has the response for the query made by agent *A2*, *A1* will directly send the response to *A2*. Even though the agents in the *request* path will not learn the result of the query, the result will reach the requester agent faster and a lot of messages can be spared. Furthermore, the agents that participated in the search, even if just for forwarding or propagating the request, can assume that, after some time, the requester agent has already received the necessary response. Hence, future similar searches (for example, an agent *A3* requesting the same contents as *A2*) can be referred to the previous requester agent (*A2*), which in turn can refer it to the responder agent (*A1*) or provide itself the response directly (to *A3*). None of the approaches cited in the related work section (see section 2) uses this technique.

3.2   Improved Flooding

To determine the effects of these techniques on the process of dynamically building a semantic overlay network, we have tested different configurations of several search mechanisms. The results of our tests show that the *flooding* algorithm has the best performance of classical approaches. Due to space limitations we will only show the results for the *flooding* algorithm. Table 1 presents the different configurations of the algorithm that we have tested.

Table 1. Configurations of the *Flooding* algorithm

Name	Description
Flooding	Agents do not cache previous searches and reply through the path where the request came from.
Improved Flooding 1	Agents do not cache previous searches and reply directly to the requester agent.
Improved Flooding 2	Agents cache previous searches, use referrals and reply through the path where the request came from.
Improved Flooding 12	Agents cache previous searches, use referrals and reply directly to the requester agent.

We have tested these different configurations of the *flooding* algorithm in an environment of 1000 agents, randomly connected to 3 neighbours each and with a *time-to-live* of 3 (each request can only be forwarded 3 times). In these tests (results are shown in Figure 1) all agents start searching for the resources that they depend on at the same time. The expression *network completeness* represents the percentage of a complete semantic overlay network that is created at a specific moment. A semantic overlay network is complete when it contains an arc for each possible dependency between any pair of resources.

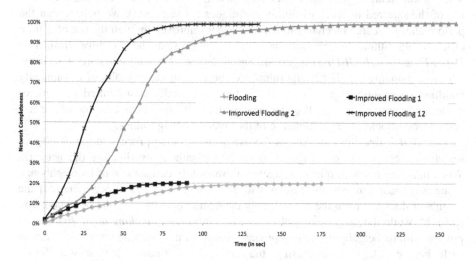

Fig. 1. Comparison of different configurations of the *Flooding* algorithm

As depicted in Figure 1, the classical configuration of the *flooding* algorithm has the worst performance of all configurations, achieving a network completeness of only 20%. The *improved flooding* 1 configuration, representing the version of the algorithm that allows agents to reply directly to the requester agent (instead of using the *request* path), presents an improvement in time performance whereas the network completeness is maintained at 20%. This allows us to conclude that the reduction in the number of messages (in consequence of the introduced variation) and consequently on the workload of each agent, is a good network evolution technique to be applied to a search algorithm. However, as we stated in section 3.1, this does not allow all contributing agents to learn the response to the request.

The *improved flooding* 2 configuration, representing the version of the algorithm that allows agents to cache information about previous searches and use referrals, has the worst time performance but a considerably better network completeness than the previous two algorithms. This shows that caching has also a positive effect on the search algorithm's overall performance, since it allows agents to take advantage of previously collected information to trigger an evolution process that will improve future searches.

The combination of all the techniques described in section 3.1 (*improved flooding* 12 configuration) presents an excellent performance (comparatively to the other configurations) both in time and network completeness. This allows us to conclude that these network evolution techniques (and especially their combination) have a very positive influence in search algorithms.

4   Efficient Search Algorithms

Even though current algorithms for unstructured networks (such as *flooding, depth-first search, random walk* and others presented in section 2) can be improved by the use of the referred network evolution techniques (in section 3), we believe that the performance of search mechanisms can be further improved through the use of a more efficient algorithm. In this section we briefly present the *Iterative Branching Depth-First Search (IBDFS)* algorithm (proposed in [17]) and compare it with the *improved flooding* 12 *(IF12)* algorithm, by showing the test results of dynamically building a semantic overlay network on top of a totally unstructured network of randomly connected agents. We also analyse how the variations of some of the test parameters influence the performance of the considered algorithms.

The *IBDFS* algorithm introduces the use of an iterative process in the *depth-first* search to increase the coverage of the network without overloading the network. When initiating a search query, an agent will randomly contact one of its neighbours. If the neighbour immediately replies with the answer, then the process ends. If the neighbour does not have the answer, then the agent contacts a second neighbour and so forth[2], while the neighbour applies the same *iterative branching depth-first* search process with its neighbours. This approach increases the branching level iteratively on each hop count, thus increasing the chances of finding the answer faster, comparatively to the *depth-first* search approach [17]. This algorithm also uses the network evolution techniques described in section 3.

4.1   Evaluation Test Results

We ran several tests for building a semantic overlay on top of a network of 1000 randomly connected agents and we compared the performance of the *IBDFS* and the *IF12* algorithms. We have limited the comparison of our proposal to the *IF12* algorithm because it was the best variation in all our tests of classic (and improved) algorithms. To fully understand the differences between the algorithms, we changed several parameters of the test configuration and analysed the effects of those variations on the performance of both algorithms.

One of the parameters that we changed was the *Time To Live (TTL)* value. Figure 2 shows the results of the variations of the *TTL* in the test (1000 agents connected to 3 neighbours each). As depicted by Figure 2, the higher the *TTL*, the higher is the difference between the performances of both algorithms. The *IBDFS* is better (in both time and network completeness) for *TTL* values greater than or equal to three. This is due to the overloading factor of the *flooding* algorithm, which gets worse as the *TTL* increases.

Another parameter that influences the performance of search algorithms is the number of neighbours that each agent is connected to at the start of the test. Figure 3 shows the results of different tests using 4 and 5 neighbours (1000 agents and a *TTL* of 3).

---

[2] See [17] for a formal description of the algorithm.

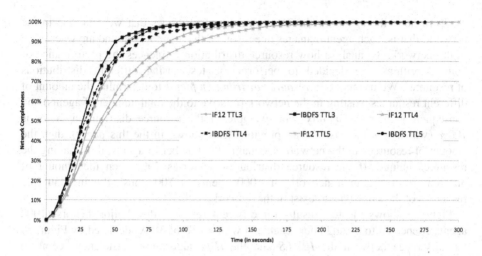

Fig. 2. Test results for variations of *TTL*

It is visible from Figure 3 that the difference between both algorithms is greater as the number of neighbours (*NN*) that each agent is connected to increases (the darker the line, the lower the number of neighbours). Again the poor performance of the *IF12* algorithm is influenced by the overloaded network (due to the increase in messages sent), which is caused by the increased number of connections from each agent. We can also see in the figure that the *IBDFS* algorithm is not affected by the change in the number of neighbours, which allows us to conclude that the algorithm is well suited for high-load and high-connectivity networks.

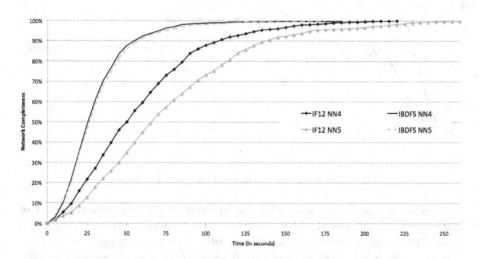

Fig. 3. Test results for variations of number of neighbours

Up to now, the agents in these tests managed resources that were unique in the network, that is, each agent manages one resource that cannot be found anywhere else in the network. To analyse how resource distribution influences the performance of both algorithms, we decided to perform the tests using different distributions of resources. We use the term *resource distribution factor* to determine the amount of different resources existing in the network (relative to the total number of agents) and consequently their availability. For example, if the resource distribution factor is 100% (which was the case for all previous tests shown in the this paper), then the amount of resources in the network is equal to the number of agents, thus making the resources unique. If the resource distribution factor is 70%, then the amount of different resources in a network of 1000 agents is 700, thus allowing multiple resources of the same type to exist in the network.

Figure 4 shows the test results for different resource distribution factors (1000 agents connected to 3 neighbours each and with a *TTL* of 3). As depicted by Figure 4, the difference between the *IBDFS* and the *IF12* algorithms' efficiency seems to increase as the resource distribution factor (*RDF*) decreases. Once again the excessive propagation and duplication of messages through the network overloads the agents with the unfruitful task of processing useless messages, which limits their capability to perform an efficient search.

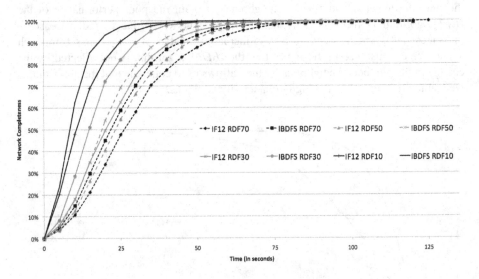

Fig. 4. Test results for variations of resources distribution

We have also performed tests with combinations of the variations presented in Figures 2-4 (*TTL*=4, *NN*=4, *RDF*=30% and *TTL*=5, *NN*=5, *RDF*=10%) and the obtained results are coherent, showing that the *IBDFS* algorithm outperforms the *IF12* algorithm both in time and network completeness. However, we cannot show the figures related to those tests due to space limitations.

5 Conclusions and Future Work

In this paper, we have shown how the efficiency of dynamically building a semantic overlay network on top of unstructured *P2P* networks can be improved by applying a set of network evolution techniques to classic search algorithms. We have also presented an efficient algorithm that outperforms the improved version of the *flooding* algorithm (the one that was shown to be the best of the tested classic algorithms), both in time and network completeness. Through an adequate balance between the network load and the learning capabilities of the presented network evolution techniques, the *Iterative Branching Depth-First Search* algorithm is a far more efficient and effective alternative to current *P2P* search algorithms for unstructured networks, especially for high-load and high-connectivity networks. These results were obtained by changing some parameters of the tests, namely the number of neighbours, the value of the *TTL* and the distribution of resources, which allowed us to determine the effects of applying the algorithms to different types of networks.

Our next steps include performing a deep analysis of the application of *IBDFS* (and certain variations of the algorithm) in dynamic networks and in large-scale networks (with hundreds of thousands of agents and resources) to determine if the algorithm still presents the same efficiency.

Acknowledgments. This work has been supported in part by the European Commission under the project grant FP6-IST-511632-CASCOM and by the Portuguese Foundation for Science and Technology under the scholarship grant SFRH/BD/27533/2006 and the funding Adetti-U[605].

References

1. Adjiman, P., Chatalic, P., Goasdoué, F., Rousset, M.-C., Laurent, S.: Distributed Reasoning in a Peer-to-Peer Setting: Application to the Semantic Web. Journal of Artificial Intelligence Research 25, 269–314 (2006)
2. Arpinar, I.B., Aleman-Meza, B., Zhang, R., Maduko, A.: Ontology-Driven Web Services Composition Platform. In: Proc. of the IEEE Int. Conf. on E-Commerce Technology, pp. 146–152. IEEE Computer Society, Washington D.C. (2004)
3. Babaoglu, O., Meling, H., Montresor, A.: Anthill: a Framework for the Development of Agent Based Peer to Peer Systems. In: Proc. IEEE ICDCS 2002, pp. 15–22 (2002)
4. Balakrishnan, H., Kaashoek, M.F., Karger, D., Morris, R., Stoica, I.: Looking Up Data in P2P Systems. Communications of the ACM 46(2), 43–48 (2003)
5. Bianchini, D., De Antonellis, V., Melchiori, M., Salvi, D.: Peer-to-Peer Semantic-Based Web Service Discovery: State of the Art. Technical Report, Dipartimento di Elettronica per l'Automazione Università di Brescia (2006)
6. Crespo, A., Garcia-Molina, H.: Routing Indices for Peer-to-Peer Systems. In: Proc of the 22nd Int. Conf. on Distributed Computing Systems, pp. 23–30 (2002)
7. Crespo, A., Garcia-Molina, H.: Semantic Overlay Networks for P2P Systems. In: Moro, G., Bergamaschi, S., Aberer, K. (eds.) AP2PC 2004. LNCS (LNAI), vol. 3601, pp. 1–13. Springer, Heidelberg (2005)
8. Dasgupta, P(R.): Improving Peer-to-Peer Resource Discovery Using Mobile Agent Based Referrals. In: Moro, G., Sartori, C., Singh, M.P. (eds.) AP2PC 2003. LNCS (LNAI), vol. 2872, pp. 186–197. Springer, Heidelberg (2004)
9. Emekci, F., Sahin, O.D., Agrawal, D., El Abbadi, A.: A Peer-to-Peer Framework for Web Service Discovery With Ranking. In: Proc. of the IEEE Int. Conf. on Web Services, pp. 192–199 (2004)

10. Ermolayev, V., Keberle, N., Plaksin, S., Terziyan, V., Kononenko, O.: Towards a Framework for Agent-Enabled Semantic Web Service Composition. International Journal of Web Service Research X (2004)
11. Fletcher, G.H.L., Sheth, H.A., Börner, K.: Unstructured Peer-to-Peer Networks: Topological Properties and Search Performance. In: Moro, G., Bergamaschi, S., Aberer, K. (eds.) AP2PC 2004. LNCS (LNAI), vol. 3601, pp. 14–27. Springer, Heidelberg (2005)
12. Gagnes, T., Plagemann, T., Munthe-Kaas, E.: A Conceptual Service Discovery Architecture for Semantic Web Services in Dynamic Environments. In: Proc. of the 22nd Int. Conf. on Data Engineering Workshops, p. 74. IEEE Computer Society, Washington, DC (2006)
13. Kalogeraki, V., Gunopulos, D., Zeinalipour-Yazti, D.: A Local Search Mechanism for Peer-to-Peer Networks. In: Proc. of the 11th Int. Conf. on Information and Knowledge Management, pp. 300–307 (2002)
14. Küngas, P., Matskin, M.: Semantic Web Service Composition Through a P2P-Based Multi-agent Environment. In: Despotovic, Z., Joseph, S., Sartori, C. (eds.) AP2PC 2005. LNCS (LNAI), vol. 4118, pp. 106–119. Springer, Heidelberg (2006)
15. Li, T.-Y., Zhao, Z.-G., You, S.-Z.: A-Peer: An Agent Platform Integrating Peer-to-Peer Network. In: Proc. of 3rd IEEE/ACM Int. Symposium on Cluster Computing and the Grid, pp. 614–617 (2003)
16. Lin, Q., Rao, R., Li, M.: DWSDM: a Web Services Discovery Mechanism Based on a Distributed Hash Table. In: Proc. of the 5th Int. Conf. on Grid and Cooperative Computing Workshops, pp. 176–180 (2006)
17. Lopes, A., Botelho, L.: Improving Multi-Agent Based Resource Coordination in Peer-to-Peer Networks. J. Networks (2008) (to appear)
18. Lv, Q., Cao, P., Cohen, E., Li, K., Shenker, S.: Search and Replication in Unstructured Peer-to-Peer Networks. In: Proc. of the 16th Int. Conf. on Supercomputing, pp. 84–95. ACM Press, New York (2002)
19. Ratnasamy, S., Francis, P., Handley, M., Karp, R., Shenker, S.: A Scalable Content Addressable Network. In: Proc. of ACM SIGCOMM 2001 Conference (2001)
20. Ratsimor, O., Chakraborty, D., Joshi, A., Finin, T., Yesha, Y.: Service Discovery in Agent-Based Pervasive Computing Environments. J. Mobile Network Applications 9(6), 679–692 (2004)
21. Risson, J., Moors, T.: Survey of Research Towards Robust Peer-to-Peer Networks: Search Methods. Comput. Networks 50(17), 3485–3521 (2006)
22. Rowstron, A., Druschel, P.: Pastry: Scalable, Decentralized Object Location, and Routing for Large-Scale Peer-to-Peer Systems. In: Guerraoui, R. (ed.) Middleware 2001. LNCS, vol. 2218, pp. 329–350. Springer, Heidelberg (2001)
23. Sheldon, M.A., Duda, A., Weiss, R., Gifford, D.K.: Discover: a Resource Discovery System Based on Content Routing. In: Proc. of the 3rd Int. World-Wide Web Conference on Technology, Tools and Applications, pp. 953–972 (1995)
24. Sivashanmugam, K., Verma, K., Sheth, V.: Discovery of Web Services in a Federated Registry Environment. In: Proc. of the IEEE Int. Conf. on Web Services, pp. 270–278 (2004)
25. Stoica, I., Morris, R., Karger, D., Kaashoek, M.F., Balakrishnan, H.: Chord: A Scalable Peer-to-Peer Lookup Service for Internet Applications. In: Proc. of the ACM SIGCOMM 2001 Conference (2001)
26. Tsoumakos, Q., Roussopoulos, N.: Adaptive Probabilistic Search for Peer-to-Peer Networks. In: Proc. of the 3rd Int. Conf. on Peer-to-Peer Computing, pp. 102–110 (2003)
27. Yang, B., Garcia-Molina, H.: Efficient Search in Peer to Peer Networks. In: Proc. of Int. Conf. on Distributed Computing Systems (2002)
28. Zhao, B.Y., Kubiatowicz, J.D., Joseph, A.D.: Tapestry: an Infrastructure for Fault-Tolerant Wide-Area Location and Routing. Technical Report. UMI Order Number: CSD-01-1141, University of California at Berkeley (2001)

A Semi-structured Overlay Network
for Large-Scale Peer-to-Peer Systems

Kousaku Kimura, Satoshi Amamiya,
Tsunenori Mine, and Makoto Amamiya

Faculty, Graduate School of ISEE., Kyushu University,
744 Motooka, Nishiku, Fukuoka 819-0395, Japan
{kimura,roger,mine,amamiya}@al.is.kyushu-u.ac.jp

Abstract. Peer-to-peer (P2P) communication and computing frameworks are important for constructing robust large-scale distributed systems. Overlay network systems use distributed hash-table (DHT) to provide scalable and efficient node search capabilities. However, the DHT-based method has a problem for the maintenance cost of dynamically changing large-scale-network, in which nodes are frequently joining and leaving. This paper proposes a novel technique of P2P communication path management. The proposed technique devises a robust semi-structured overlay network called Ordered Tree with Tuft (OTT for short). OTT provides not only efficient node searching, but also low-cost self-maintenance capabilities for the dynamically changing network. In this method, joining and leaving of a node are managed in $O(1)$ with high probability. Furthermore, the proposed OTT-based technique can find and construct a path shorter than that on the normal ordered tree, by setting up bypass links between remote nodes on OTT.

1 Introduction

Peer-to-peer (P2P) message communication and computing techniques are important to develop large-scale distributed systems. Multiagent systems, in which agents are distributed over the large scale network like Internet, particularly need a flexible P2P message communication environment.

Various P2P systems have been proposed so far. For instance, Gnutella [1] and Freenet [2] are in practical use for file exchange and Skype [3] is used as the IP telephone system. In P2P systems, every node is connected only to a few neighbor nodes, and, for sending a message to a distant node, the sender node asks neighbor nodes to relay the message to the destination node. In this framework, it is important for the P2P system in dynamically changing network to guarantee the soundness in that the message arrives at the destination in safe.

Various kinds of DHT-based P2P algorithms [4][5][6][7][8][9][10][11][12] are proposed to solve the problem by configuring the structured overlay network. In these methods, assuming a key is given, each node or content is mapped onto the structure to optimize the performance of contents search. The search cost in these methods is $O(\log N)$ for the N-node network. In DHT, when a node joins

D. Beneventano et al. (Eds.): AP2PC 2008/2009, LNAI 6573, pp. 83–94, 2012.

or leaves the network, its neighbor node has to be selected and its routing table has to be modified to maintain the routing paths in the structured network. If the node fails to keep track of the change, the search process will take more time or the search will be in failure. In general, as the network is larger, the maintenance cost becomes higher. For the large-scale network, the maintenance will become the bottleneck when many nodes frequently join and leave. This bottleneck is serious in practical networks. If the maintenance procedure spreads over the network and thus takes more time, the search will frequently fail. If the maintenance can rapidly be done without spreading over the network, the search can be safer and the network will be more robust.

This paper proposes a semi-structured overlay network which uses a new network topology called Ordered Tree with Tuft (OTT for short) to solve the problem of the maintenance cost for the dynamically changing large-scale network. Assuming every node of OTT to be given a unique ID, OTT is configured as an ordered tree according to the ID. Each node of the ordered tree has a set of ring structured nodes, which is called a **tuft**. Furthermore, each node setups a bypassing route by caching its neighbor node on bypassing route that has been used in the previous communication. Each node of OTT maintains its neighbor nodes, and if one of the neighbor nodes is lost, it searches other paths and updates its neighbor nodes on the paths. The OTT method is effective in performance-by-cost of the route maintenance, because each node can maintain in $O(1)$ with high probability as long as tufts remain. and can find paths to a destination node, whose length is much less than $\log N$ for OTT with N nodes in practical use.

This paper describes the structure of OTT, and gives the method of message routing, path searching and routing table maintenance. The evaluation by software simulation is shown and discussed.

2   Structure of OTT

OTT is an overlay network configured on the physical network (e.g. TCP/IP network). OTT is constructed with an ordered tree and ringed tufts. The ringed tuft is attached to each node of the ordered tree. Figure 1 (left) shows an example of OTT. We call the node of the ordered tree **a tree-node** and the node of the ringed tuft **a ring-node**.

OTT takes advantage of features of the ordered tree structure and the ring structure. The complexity of node insertion, deletion and search are $O(\log N)$ in the ordered tree with N nodes. In contrast, for the ring of size M, the complexity is $O(1)$ for both node insertion and deletion and $O(M)$ for search.

2.1   ID and Adjacent Table

Every OTT node has a unique ID. The ID is given as a tuple of hashed values (u, v). The left child of each tree-node has a u value smaller than that of the parent tree-node, and the right child has a u value larger than that of the

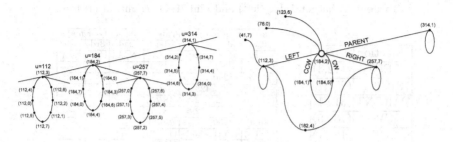

Fig. 1. Example of OTT (left) and connected nodes of (184,2) (right)

parent tree-node. Each tree-node has a ringed tuft. All nodes in the tuft have the same u value as its tree-node, and each of the ring-nodes is identified by its v value. Each node carries an Adjacent Table (AT for short) and a Link Table (LT for short) in order to maintain P2P communication paths on OTT. AT holds IDs of adjacent nodes in OTT, i.e. parent node (PARENT), left child node (LEFT), right child node (RIGHT), clockwise adjacent node in the ring (CW) and counter clockwise adjacent node in the ring (CCW). Figure 1 (right) and table 1 (left) show an example of OTT and AT for the node $(184, 2)$, respectively.

2.2   Link Table (LT)

LT is used for message routing and path searching. All connections of each node are held in LT. Successor nodes held in LT are on the path to its destination. Each LT entry holds several candidates of successor node to the same destination. Thus, every node holds multiple routes to the same destination, and if the current route does not work in some reason, another successor node is selected from the stored candidates. Note that all nodes in AT are also held in LT.

LT also holds successor nodes other than adjacent nodes. We call such a node **a bypass node**. The number of bypass nodes is set to low ratio of the number of the whole LT entries. If the number of bypass nodes is set to the larger, the shorter path will be found, but path search messages will increase and flood over OTT. Therefore the number of bypass nodes should be decided at the practical usage of OTT[1]. Table 1 (right) shows the LT of the node $(184, 2)$.

2.3   Path Search and Min-Max Value

Naive Path Search Method. When a sender node holds no path information to a destination node, the sender node searches and sets up the path information to the destination. The search process begins at the sender node. Suppose the ID of the destination node is (u_d, v_d). The search message is delivered to its successor nodes, i.e. adjacent nodes and bypass nodes. When a successor node n_0 with ID

---

[1] In our experiment, the number of bypass nodes is set from 16 to 32 for the whole numbers of LT entries between 1024 and 8192.

Table 1. Adjacent Table (left) and Link Table (right) of (184,2)

Direction	ID
LEFT	(112,3)
RIGHT	(257,7)
PARENT	(314,1)
CW	(184,5)
CCW	(184,1)

Desti- nation	min-max value	Candidate successor nodes			
		1st	2nd	3rd	4th
self	< 82, 272 >	N/A	N/A	N/A	N/A
(112,3)	< 82, 135 >	(112,3)	-	-	-
(257,7)	< 240, 272 >	(257,7)	-	-	-
(314,1)	< 82, 423 >	(314,1)	-	-	-
(184,5)	< 82, 272 >	(184,5)	-	-	-
(184,1)	< 82, 272 >	(184,1)	-	-	-
(76,0)	< 50, 78 >	(76,0)	-	-	-
(123,6)	< 121, 125 >	(123,6)	-	-	-
(41,7)	-	(112,3)	-	-	-
(182,4)	-	(257,7)	(112,3)	-	-

(u_0, v_0) receives the message, it checks whether $u_d = u_0$. If $u_d = u_0$ then search message is delivered into ringed tuft and each ring-node checks whether $v_d = v_0$. Otherwise, the search message is delivered to the left child node if $u_d < u_0$, or to the right child node if $u_d > u_0$.

At the same time, the search message will be delivered to its parent node. In this search process, each node will receive the same search message multiple times. In order to avoid redundant search message propagation, each node, when receiving the same search message, discards the redundant message.

Efficient Path Search with Min-Max Value. If the search message is delivered to all the adjacent and bypass nodes, the search messages will flood over OTT. In order to avoid the flooding, we make each tree-node hold a pair of minimum and maximum of u values of its subtree. We call it the min-max value. Suppose a node n_0 has its own u value u_0 and the min-max value $[u_{0-min}, u_{0-max}]$. When the node n_0 receives the search message to the destination node n_d whose ID is (u_d, v_d), if $u_d < u_{0-min} \lor u_{0-max} < u_d$ the node n_0 never delivers the search message into its subtree, because the the target node n_d is not in the subtree. Thus, the flooding of useless search messages is suppressed.

The min-value (max-value) is set to the min-value (max-value) of its left (right) child. If the node has no left (right) child it is set to the u value of the node itself. When the left or right child is replaced with another node or changes its min-max value, the min-max value is recalculated, and the new value is transmitted to all the connected nodes.

3   Protocols

The topology of OTT keeps down the reconstructing cost for a dynamically changing network in which nodes frequently join and leave. In this reconstruction process, mini-max value calculation and its updating messages are refrained from spreading out beyond the neighbor nodes. In the following description, we assume that every node of OTT is assigned to a distributed platform, which is connected to a physical network (e.g. Internet), and every procedure on the node runs on its platform[2].

---

[2] In our case, multiagent Kodama[13] is used as the platform.

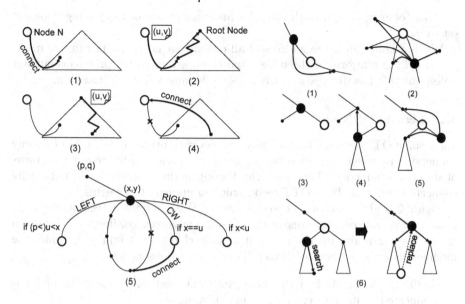

Fig. 2. Join (left) and Leave (right) procedure

3.1   Joining of Node

When joining, a new node searches its position in OTT using its ID. In the course of the search, the min-max value of each node is updated if necessary. Figure 2 (left) depicts the procedure when a new node joins OTT. The detail of the procedure is as follows:

(1) When joining OTT, the joining node is connected to another node on a list given by a bootstrap node like [7] or a Web server.
(2) The joining node sends the search message, which consists of its address and ID, toward the OTT root node.
(3) The search message is transmitted from the root through tree-nodes of OTT until the appropriate position to insert the node is found. When a tree-node n_0 receives the message, it compares the u value of the joining node (say u_j) with that of itself (say u_0). If $u_j = u_0$ then the appropriate position to insert the node is found. Otherwise, if $u_j > u_0$ (or $u_j < u_0$), the search message is sent to the right (or left) child node.
(4) When the position is found, the joining node is re-connected from that position and disconnects the node which was connected at the step (1).
(5) Furthermore, the joining node is placed between the tree-node and the right next ring-node. At the same time, the min-(or max-)value of the node n_0 is replaced with u_j if $u_j <$ min-value (or $u_j >$ max-value).

If the tree-node of $u_j = u_0$ is not found, the joining node is a virgin. In this case, the virgin node is connected to the leaf tree-node as its right (or left) child if

$u_j > u_0$ (or if $u_j < u_0$). Both the min- and max-values of the joining node are set to u_j.

When a node joins, the address of all co-existent nodes in its tuft are memorized (in the platform of the node), and the position search process is cut out unless the tuft has disappeared when the node once left out joins again.

3.2 Leaving of Node

We assume OTT uses TCP as its physical network protocol. OTT has two-way connection between connected nodes, and every node can figure out the status of its connected node. Therefore, the leaving node is quickly detected by its connected nodes, and the OTT reconstruction immediately begins.[3]

Figure 2 (right) depicts six cases of leaving. When a node detects its adjacent node is leaving, it performs one of the following actions according to the position of the leaving node. In any cases, if a node changes its min-max value, the modified value is notified to all its adjacent and bypass nodes.

(1) If the leaving node is a ring-node, its right next ring-node (CW node) is connected to its left next ring-node (CCW node).
(2) If the leaving node is a non-leaf tree-node and has its tuft, the right next ring-node comes to the position of the tree-node and the replaced node is connected to its left next ring-node (CCW), left child (LEFT), right child (RIGHT) and parent (PARENT) tree-nodes.
(3) If the leaving node is a leaf and has no tuft, nothing is done.
(4) If the leaving node is a tree-node with only one child and has no tuft, its child node comes to the position of the tree-node, and the replaced node is connected to its parent tree-node (PARENT).
(5) If the leaving node is a tree-node with both children and has no tuft, then, if its right (or left) child has no child, the right (or left) child is connected to the parent (PARENT) and left (or right) child (LEFT (or RIGHT)) tree-node of the leaving node.
(6) Otherwise, the node with the largest u value is searched in the left subtree and comes to the position of the leaving node, and the connection of the replaced node is modified.

In the above procedure, each node notifies the information of its AT to the nodes registered in its AT and LT so that the nodes keep the connection information. By this, when a node leaves, only its adjacent nodes reconstruct their connections, except for the case (6), as shown in Figure 2 (right). The case (6) requires search for a node which has the greatest u value in the subtree. occurs. However the case (3), (4), (5) and (6) will seldom occur as long as OTT never declines so much as tufts disappear.

Even if a node happens to be in the case that all its successor nodes disappear, the node will be able to take the join procedure as a virgin node.

---

[3] If the UDP connection is used, periodical confirmation of the node status is required. In this case, detection of node leaving from the network might be delayed.

3.3   Routing

When sending a message to a destination node, the sender node issues the message to its highest-ranked successor node. If the successor node returns no acknowledge, the next highest-ranked successor is chosen and tried again.

The successor node, when received the message, checks whether the node itself is the targeted destination. If true, the the routing process terminates. Otherwise the successor node relays the message to its highest-ranked successor node. This message relaying continues until the message arrives at the destination node. If any path to the destination is broken off, the failure message is returned to the sender node, and the sender node conducts the path search.

3.4   Path Search

The path search is conducted by two methods: a normal-ordered-tree search and flooding-and-subtree search. The normal-ordered-tree search is carried out on OTT without using bypass links. The flooding-and-subtree search repeatedly issues a search message, using bypass links on OTT, from node to node until the value of TTL (Time To Live) becomes 0.

Assume here the ID of the targeted destination node n_d is (u_d, v_d). When a node n_0 receives the search message, n_0 performs the following procedure:

(1) If the node n_0 is the destination, i.e. $(u_0, v_0) = (u_d, v_d)$, the node returns the success answer to the sender node.
(2) Otherwise, if the node n_0 is directly connected to the destination node n_d , it sends the message to n_d .
(3) Otherwise, if $u_0 = u_d \wedge v_0 \neq v_d$, the node n_0 passes the message to the right next ring-node in its tuft to search the node n_d with v_d.
(4) Otherwise, if the node n_0 finds the successor node n_s from the candidate successor nodes (say n_i's) in LT, n_0 sends the message to node n_s. Here, the node n_s has the min-max value $[u_{s-min}, u_{s-max}]$ such that
$$(u_{s-min} \leq u_d \leq u_{s-max}) \wedge (u_{s-max} - u_{s-min} = \min\{u_{i-max} - u_{i-min}\}).$$
(5) Otherwise,
  (a) When performing the normal-ordered-tree search, the node n_0 sends the message to its adjacent nodes held in AT: If n_0 is a tree-node, it sends to the PARENT node, or if n_0 is a ring-node, sends to the CW node. TTL value is not counted in this search.
  (b) When performing the flooding-and-subtree search, if $TTL > 0$, n_0 sends the message to all the bypass nodes after decrementing TTL.

The difference between the normal-ordered-tree search and the flooding-and-subtree search is only in step (5), which, however, makes considerable difference in performance. If we use the two methods at the same time, the search is sound and can find a shorter path, even though it might make the search cost higher. Furthermore, by combining two methods, multiple paths can be found, and each node on the paths can select several successor nodes on the shortest path and registers them in LT as the highest-ranked successor candidates.

4   Evaluation

We implemented a software simulator of the OTT method and evaluated for a large-scale network of $4194304(= 2^{22})$ nodes.

In the simulation, the node ID is given by the following ID allocation strategy: The maximum ring size is set to m. When a new node is created, if the ring size is less than m then its ID is set to the same u value as its tree-node and a unique v value in the tuft ring. Otherwise, another u value is selected. In the evaluation, we set $m = 8$, and the ratio of tree-node size to the total ring-node size is 1 to 7. For instance, in the OTT of 128 nodes, the number of tree-nodes is 16, and the total number of ring-nodes is 112 $(= 7 * 16)$. In the following discussion, we use two parameters N and B, where N is the number of nodes in OTT, and B the number of bypass links of each node, respectively. Each node makes B bypass links to nodes chosen randomly.

4.1   Cost Performance

First, we evaluate the maintenance cost and path search cost. Here, the cost is defined as the total number of message transfers occurred between nodes during link connection, link disconnection and communication.

Here, N is the number of tree-nodes, B is the number of the bypass links held in a node, and k is the average number of nodes needed to modify their min-max value.

Joining of Node. The cost of each step in the joining process described in Section 3.1 is estimated on average as: 1 for the step (1), $\log N$ for the step (2), $2 \log N + k \times B$ for the step (3), 1 for the step (4) and 1 for the step (5) when the joined node is a tree-node or 2 when the joined node is a ring-node.

Figure 3 (left) plots the maintenance cost for the first time joining nodes (virgin nodes), where N varies from $128(= 2^7)$ to $4194304(= 2^{22})$ and $B=16$, 24, 32. The figure shows that the cost is almost proportional to logarithm of the number of nodes, e.g. it is about 110 when $N = 2^{22}$ and $B = 32$. This figure also shows that k is about 2 since the cost of node joining is $2 \log N + kB$, where $2 \log N$ is the cost of normal-ordered-tree search and kB is the cost of min-max value transmission with bypass links, e.g. it is about 2×32 when $B = 32$.

The maintenance cost for re-joining node is $O(1)$, since the position search is cut out unless the tuft has disappeared (see Section 3.1). Figure 4 (left) plots the ratio of survived tufts in the OTT of $N = 2^{22}$, when the leaving node is successively selected at random. This figure shows that only 2% of tufts have disappeared even when a half of 2^{22} nodes have left. Therefore, the maintenance cost for rejoining node is very low, almost $O(1)$ when more than a half of nodes are alive.

Leaving of Node. The cost of each step in the node leaving process described in Section 3.2 is estimated as: 1 for the step (1), 4 for the step (2), 0 for the step (3), 1 for the step (4), 2 for the step (5) and $\log M_{sub} + \alpha$ for the step (6).

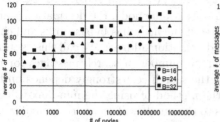
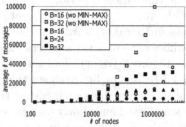

Fig. 3. Average maintenance cost for the first-time joining node (left) and Average cost of path search (right)

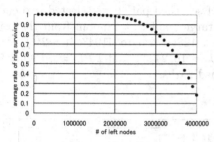
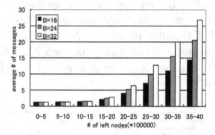

Fig. 4. The ratio of survived tufts in OTT of size 2^{22} nodes (left) and average maintenance cost for the leaving node selected at random and withdrawn from the OTT of 2^{22} nodes (right)

Here, M_{sub} is the number of nodes in the subtree of the leaving node, and α is the cost to the leaving node that has the largest u value and at most 4. Note that the cost of min-max value transmission is not included in this estimation.

Figure 4 (right) plots the average cost per 500,000 times when the leaving node is successively selected at random from the OTT with $N = 2^{22}$ and $B = 16, 24, 32$. Note that the cost of min-max value transmission is included in this simulation data. This figure shows that the cost is kept very low until a half of 2^{22} nodes has left out. Most of nodes need not reconfigure the ordered tree because their tufts exist. When more than half of nodes withdrew, the number of tree-nodes without tuft increases and the cost becomes higher.

Path Search. In the path search evaluation, the pair of sender and receiver nodes is selected at random, and path searching is tried 10000 times for each pair on the OTT of the size of N from $2^7(= 128)$ to $2^{22}(= 4194304)$. Figure 3 (right) depicts the average search cost with and without min-max value. The two methods of the normal-ordered-tree search and the flooding-and-subtree search are simultaneously performed. The cost of the normal-ordered-tree search is $O(2 \log N + 8)$ since the cost of climbing up and down on the ordered tree is $O(2 \log N)$ and the number of ring-nodes of each tree-node is 8. In contrast, the cost of flooding-and-subtree search is $O(B^{TTL})$ when the number of bypass links is B. The simulation is performed for the case of $TTL=3$ and $B=16, 24, 32$. In the search process, even if TTL becomes 0 at some node, the destination search continues further downward to its subtree if the node has bypass links and child nodes whose mini-max value covers the destination address. We call this "subtree search." Figure 3 (right) plots the average number of search messages for the case of $TTL=3$. The figure shows that the search cost strongly depends on the flooding. However, the search cost of the method of using the min-max value is largely suppressed and slowly increases to the number of nodes, compared to the method without using the min-max value.

4.2   Path Length

In order to measure the average length of searched paths, we selected two end nodes, search-message-sender node and target node, at random from the set of OTT nodes of size of N ranging from $128(=2^7)$ to $4194304(=2^{22})$. We measured it 10000 times for each N, for $B = 16, 24, 32$, and $TTL = 3$. Figure 5 (left) depicts the average length of searched paths.

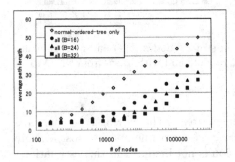 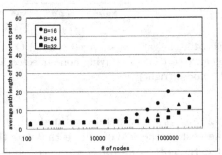

Fig. 5. Average path length(left) and average length of the shortest path(right)

This figure shows that the average length of the paths searched by the normal-ordered-tree search is about $2 \log N$ and is longer than that of paths searched by both the normal-ordered-tree and the flooding-and-subtree searches. Figures 5(right) shows the average length of the shortest path.[4] These results show the effect of the flooding-and-subtree search.

5   Related Work

Overlay networks for the P2P systems are classified to structured and unstructured ones. Gnutella [1] and Freenet [2] are the unstructured networks. Unstructured overlay networks mainly employ flooding method for node searching.

---

[4] In the simulation, the path of shortest turnaround time is selected.

The flooding method has advantages in the point that each node does not have to maintain link connections and the searcher node can receive multiple answers. However, the search is not complete because the search message can not be assured to reach the destination if the TTL is set to a limit to prevent the flooding of search messages.

DHT is one of the most popular methods for structured overlay networks, and various kinds of network configurations are proposed: circle [4], hypercube [7], n-ary tree [5] , B-tree [9][10], butterfly network [11], de Bruijn Graph [12], and so on. Node searching in DHT is complete and its cost is $O(\log N)$. In addition, the processing load is well balanced among nodes because the nodes and contents are evenly scattered. However, DHT is harder to make the search flexible compared to the unstructured network. Although the path length is $O(\log N)$ in DHT, the number of hops does not necessarily mean the network proximity. Therefore, we have to devise the choice mechanism of routes, i.e. the choice of neighbor nodes and ID [14] , by considering the network proximity. In addition, each node have to maintain its bypass link table of size $O(\log N)$ whenever a new node joins or an existing node leaves. As the network becomes larger, the maintenance cost will become higher, and at worst, the search will fall into failure because of the time consuming maintenance [15].

Our method devised on the OTT-based semi-structured overlay network has advantages both the unstructured and structured networks. The flexible and efficient path finding is obtained by applying both the normal-ordered-tree search and the flooding-and-subtree search to the OTT-structure. The network is robust because each node can maintain in $O(1)$ with high probability if ring tufts remain. This will occur until half of OTT nodes leave the network. In addition, choosing the first found route in path searching, we can take into account the network proximity.

6 Conclusion

This paper proposed a novel technique of P2P communication path management. The proposed technique devises a robust semi-structured overlay network called OTT (Ordered Tree with Tuft). The OTT method is effective in performance-by-cost of the route maintenance for dynamically changing network. The effect of the OTT method is evaluated by software simulation. The simulation result shows that the maintenance cost is $O(1)$ with high probability if a half of nodes in OTT is alive (except for the first joining), and can find one or more paths to a destination node, whose length is much less than $\log N$ for N nodes in practical use, while the path search cost goes up to B^{TTL} in the worst case. Therefore, we can say that OTT keeps robustness by performing the quick maintenance of OTT when a half of nodes in the network is alive. In addition, the flooding-and-subtree search successfully finds short-length paths on OTT by using bypass links.

This method is implemented as an overlay network in Kodama [13] system. As an application of Kodama we are developing a business matching and collaboration support system. In this system, each node delivers and receives business plans and company information. Therefore it needs robust overlay network.

Further research issue is to develop the distributed node ID allocation method. The node ID allocation was performed as a centralized process in the simulation. But the ID allocation process should be performed in the distributed environment. Another one is the more precise simulation to reflect practical application. The simulation of this paper separately performed the node join, leave and search processes. However, these three processes will occur concurrently in the practical network services. Therefore the simulation is needed for more realistic dynamic network environments where the node join, leave and search processes occur in a highly concurrent way.

References

1. Gnutella: The gnutella protocol specification v0.4 (2000), http://www.gnutella.com/
2. Clarke, I., Sandberg, O., Wiley, B., Hong, T.W.: Freenet: A Distributed Anonymous Information Storage and Retrieval System. In: The Workshop on Design Issues in Anonymity and Unobservablity, pp. 46–66 (2000)
3. web site, http://www.skype.com/
4. Stoica, I., Morris, R., Karger, D., Kaashoek, F., Balakrishnan, H.: Chord: A scalable Peer-To-Peer Lookup Service for Internet Applications. In: The 2001 ACM SIGCOMM Conference, pp. 149–160 (2001)
5. Rowstron, A., Druschel, P.: Pastry: Scalable, Decentralized Object Location, and Routing for Large-Scale Peer-to-Peer Systems. In: Guerraoui, R. (ed.) Middleware 2001. LNCS, vol. 2218, pp. 329–350. Springer, Heidelberg (2001)
6. Zhao, B.Y., Kubiatowicz, J.D., Joseph, A.D.: Tapestry: An infrastructure for fault-tolerant wide-area location and routing. Technical Report UCB/CSD-01-1141, UC Berkeley (2001)
7. Ratnasamy, S., Francis, P., Handley, M., Karp, R., Shenker, S.: A scalable content addressable network. Technical Report TR-00-010, Berkeley, CA (2000)
8. Maymounkov, P., Mazières, D.: Kademlia: A Peer-to-Peer Information System Based on the XOR Metric. In: Druschel, P., Kaashoek, M.F., Rowstron, A. (eds.) IPTPS 2002. LNCS, vol. 2429, pp. 53–65. Springer, Heidelberg (2002)
9. Baquero, C., Lopes, N.: B+tree on p2p: Providing content indexing over dht overlays. Technical report, Universidade do Minho (2004)
10. Prakash, A.C.: P-Tree: A P2P Index for Resource Discovery Applications. In: 13th International World Wide Web Conference, pp. 390–391 (May 2004)
11. Malkhi, D., Naor, M., Ratajzcak, D.: Viceroy: Scalable emulation of butterfly networks for distributed hash tables (2003)
12. Kaashoek, M.F., Karger, D.R.: Koorde: A Simple Degree-Optimal Distributed Hash Table. In: Kaashoek, M.F., Stoica, I. (eds.) IPTPS 2003. LNCS, vol. 2735, pp. 323–336. Springer, Heidelberg (2003)
13. Zhong, G., Amamiya, S., Takahashi, K., Mine, T., Amamiya, M.: The Design and Implementation of KODAMA System. IEICE Transactions INF E85-D, 637–646 (2002)
14. Song, J., Park, S., Yang, J.: An Adaptive Proximity Route Selection Scheme in DHT-Based Peer to Peer Systems. In: Liew, K.-M., Shen, H., See, S., Cai, W. (eds.) PDCAT 2004. LNCS, vol. 3320, pp. 778–781. Springer, Heidelberg (2004)
15. Rhea, S., Geels, D., Roscoe, T., Kubiatowicz, J.: Handling Churn in a DHT. In: The 2004 USENIX Technical Conference (2004)

The Future of Energy Markets and the Challenge of Decentralized Self-management

Frances Brazier[1], Elth Ogston[2], and Martijn Warnier[1]

[1] Intelligent Interactive Distributed Systems*,
VU University, Amsterdam,
The Netherlands
{FMT.Brazier,M.Warnier}@few.vu.nl
[2] Department of Computer Science,
University of Warwick,
United Kingdom
elth@dcs.warwick.ac.uk

Abstract. Complex, intelligent, distributed systems in dynamic environments, such as the power grid need to be designed to adapt autonomously. Self-management, in particular of large scale adaptive systems such as the power grid, is necessarily distributed. Agent and peer-to-peer based decentralized self-management can change the future of energy markets in which the power grid plays a core role.

Assuming that both consumers and providers of energy are autonomous systems, represented by software agents or peers capable of self-management, virtual organizations of systems can emerge and adapt when necessary. Communication structures between systems, e.g., hierarchical or clustered organizations, can emerge, organizations between and within which systems can choose to cooperate and coordinate their actions, or compete. Overlay structures (as defined within p2p research) define such adaptive communication structures, multi-agent research provides interaction patterns. Global goals are achieved by local management on the basis of local goals and knowledge. The appropriate delegation of managerial responsibility determines the control structure. Aggregate information differs depending on the position of a system in an organization, the aggregation mechanisms and policies.

1   Introduction

Complex, intelligent, distributed systems in large-scale dynamic environments need to be designed to adapt. Self-management, in particular of large scale adaptive systems such as the power grid, is necessarily distributed. Agent and peer-to-peer based decentralized self-management can change the future of energy markets in which the power grid plays a core role. Agent and peer-to-peer based decentralized self-management can change the future of energy markets.

---

* As of September 1 2009 the IIDS group will be part of the Systems Engineering group, Faculty of Technology, Policy and Management, Delft University of Technology.

D. Beneventano et al. (Eds.): AP2PC 2008/2009, LNAI 6573, pp. 95–103, 2012.

Energy markets contain vast numbers of systems/devices that produce and consume electricity. These systems/devices are distributed across many inter-connected networks, both physical and organizational, each with their own local service requirements. They operate in a complex and ever changing physical environment, and must serve the needs of a highly autonomous user group.

Decentralized self-management is the approach this paper explores. Emer-gent virtual organizations with local knowledge are needed to structure, and thus reduce, the complexity of global management tasks. Within these organiza-tions, interaction protocols are needed for systems to coordinate their individual behaviors.

The total power generated by a grid, for example, must be related to the total demand, taking constraints on the transport network into account. The better this management task is performed, the more efficient the system is as a whole. In the ideal case all systems connected to a grid coordinate their plans for energy production and use, continuously adapting to take into account the changing constraints imposed by their environment and users, with minimal overhead and performance loss.

Dynamic management on the scale of an electrical grid of smart devices raises a number of key challenges with respect to most effective virtual organizations:

– *Creating and maintaining multi-level dynamic virtual organizations*

Communication Structures

Overlay structures define connections between agents: communication net-works. These networks need to adapt to change in their dynamic environ-ment. They also need to be maintained. They define the potential paths for dissemination and aggregation of information. Communication structures include (1) hierarchical networks, (2) semi-clustered hierarchical networks, (3) clustered network, or (4) fully unstructured networks, as depicted be-low in Figures 1-4. Which network structure is most appropriate for which application under which conditions is an important research question. The value of multi-level communication structures with different communication structures at different levels within an organization for different purposes, is currently a topic of research. Other research questions include determining the ideal number of systems within each network, membership criteria of networks, and recognizing when group membership should change.

– *Division of management responsibility within a multi-level dynamic virtual organization*

Control

Given one or more global goals, determining which appropriate local goals can be negotiated with/delegated to specific systems within an organization is a challenge. Which level of authority should be assigned to which network

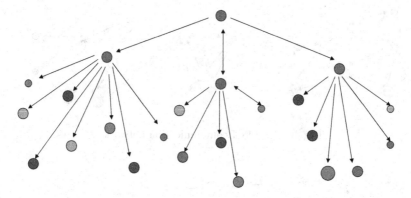

Fig. 1. Hierarchical network structure

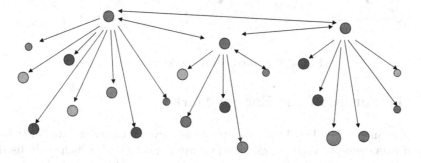

Fig. 2. Semi-structured communication network

within a virtual organization? Which is most effective? Which systems can be assigned which level of authorization?

– *Creating and maintaining multi-level dynamic virtual organizations*

Aggregation of Information

A system's location within a communication structure determines the information it can access and process, its local knowledge of system behavior. Aggregation policies and mechanisms define which information can be known where and when. Research questions include: What is the appropriate algorithm for aggregation of information? And how does simplifying or increasing the complexity of a management task at one level effect the complexity of management at other levels?

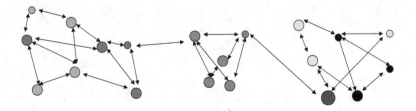

Fig. 3. Clustered communication network

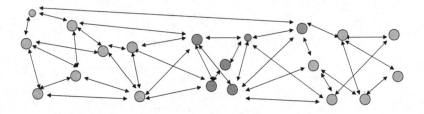

Fig. 4. Unstructured network structures

2   The Future of the Energy Market

The scale and highly distributed nature of the power grid necessitates distribution of management. Virtual organizations are a means with which such distribution can be regulated: the communication structure, distribution of control, distribution of managerial responsibility.

Demand for electricity is, for the most part, although partially predictable, not controllable, and storage capacity is limited. Currently the only solution to fluctuations in demand, limited flexibility of large power plants, and strict global reliability requirements, is for providers to have more power produced than strictly necessary with a higher capacity than most often required.

Recent technological developments, however, are opening new possibilities for improving power grid management. Ubiquitous communications networks and low-cost controllers may provide the flexibility the market needs. Improvements in solar panels, domestic-sized wind turbines, and micro-CHP, and the increasingly widespread availability of high capacity batteries in devices such as electric vehicles change how and where power is most efficiently generated and stored. Current grid management systems are, however, limited in scale by their use of partially centralized decision making. Wholesale markets use a centralized clearinghouse to calculate and distribute prices and to inform participants of winning and losing bids. This means that only large power plants and utilities participate in electricity markets. To incorporate larger numbers of participants, further decentralization is required. Research on distributed electricity resource management (DER) addresses this problem[1,2,3], bringing together and furthering research on peer-to-peer and multi-agent systems.

3   Challenges of Decentralized Self-management

Distributed energy resource management is a challenge: self management the solution proposed. This section highlights some of our research efforts in this area.

3.1   Distributed Self-management of Individual Appliances: Communication and Aggregation

Virtual organizations of agents define communication structures between agents, e.g., hierarchical organizations [4], between and within which agents can choose to cooperate and coordinate their actions, or compete. Dynamic organized hierarchies [5] can be used to support adaptive, aggregate, nonlinear behavior, as a means to reduce complexity. Coordination in unstructured environments entails distributed search and distributed scheduling [6,7].

Our current research in this area focuses on the level of individual appliances. Global stabilization of the energy consumption of an electricity network (power grid), by minimizing oscillations of all thermostatic controlled appliances (TCA) within a single household, is the goal. Such devices, for example, refrigerators, air conditioners and water heaters, consume 25% of the total energy supply in the USA [8]. Self management of these devices could potentially have a significant effect on the stabilization of global resource consumption. To this purpose software agents in TCAs autonomously and automatically negotiate their resource requirements, configurations, and SLAs, ultimately acquiring global stabilization in energy consumption, which in turn leads to higher reliability of the power grid and lower costs for consumers and producers.

This study [9] proposes a fully decentralized agent-based approach to global stabilization of resource utilization, for energy consumption, based on local coordination. The approach is threefold and can be outlined as follows: (i) Agents are members of a hierarchical virtual organization, structuring agent interactions and aggregation of agent resource requirements. (ii) A simple agent knowledge model is assumed on the basis of which resource requests are generated. (iii) Agents can make local adaptive decisions on the basis of information they receive from the agents to which they are linked. This research focuses on minimizing the oscillations of thermostatic controlled appliances. Software agents autonomously negotiate their resource requirements and configuration [10,11].

Using relatively straightforward models of energy devices this research [9] has shown that hierarchical local coordination achieves emerging convergence of the global stabilization through local knowledge, local decisions and local interactions by individual software agents. Self-management has thus shown to be feasible, as demonstrated in agent-based simulations, in the AgentScape [12] platform. The hierarchical organization plays an important role in the proposed

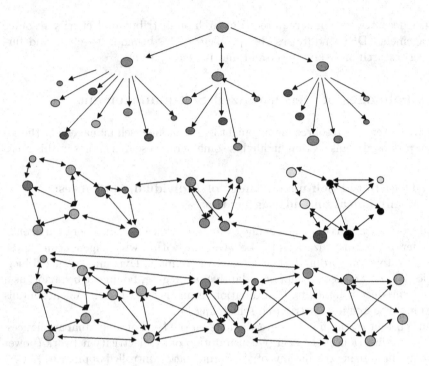

Fig. 5. Layered network structures

method. Current research therefore focuses on peer-to-peer based self-managed robust hierarchical topologies designed to adapt to local failures, reorganizing the topology as needed on the basis of local knowledge.

In [13] an approach for building such robust hierarchical topologies is investigated. The approach is based on a 3-layer communication overlay architecture for self-organization. Figure 5 depicts the approach. Communication *between* the different network layers (as one depends on the other) is not depicted, but is a essential to the approach.

3.2 Self Management in Virtual Power Stations: Managerial Responsibility

How management can be most effectively divided between parties in distributed energy resource management problems is another issue our research addresses. Virtual power stations consisting of a large number of nodes, such as office buildings, each with a small amount of generating capacity group together to form an entity that can participate in an electricity market [1,14]. Control agents on each node manage local resources and interact with each other to achieve global goals. In our research a scenario based on the measured output of a photovoltaic installation in Newcastle, NSW, Australia, and price data taken from the

Australian National Electricity Market has been used to study different management options. The amount of profit that may be realized under different forms of distributed management in realistic operating conditions has been compared.

There are many ways in which a resource management task, like that encountered in DER and in this scenario, can be divided between locations. Methods can be classified by where final authority for resource use is located. Authority can lie with a central overseer, for instance as commonly used in computational grids to plan and allocate jobs so as to make optimal use of a set of processors. Alternatively, management can be decentralized, with each node having authority over its own resources, as is often the goal in multi-agent systems which aim to maximize node autonomy. Or central and local managers can have complimentary tasks, as in many peer-to-peer systems where a central controller manages the composition of mostly independent groups of nodes, but within groups nodes have control of their local resources.

Which of the above methods of apportioning control is most appropriate depends upon diverse application requirements, including the degree to which the desired behavior differs from the systems natural behavior, the sensitivity of the system to parameter variations, and the independence required by individual components in order to be able to accommodated local constraints [15,16].

Understanding how various distributed management schemes influence achievable profit in a virtual power station is important because the form of distributed management employed has consequences for the required communication and computation infrastructure. Strong central coordination requires powerful servers. Frequent or precise coordination requires high capacity, reliable communication links. Advanced self-management techniques require system monitoring as well as complex devices on which to run local control agents. The benefit of a management scheme may therefore be outweighed by the cost of implementing it.

Simulation experiments testing the ways these forms of management can be combined to control a virtual power station have shown that each has an important role to play. However, the quality of management in each case is less important. Weak management techniques have shown to provide substantial increases in profit. Increasing the quality of management, on the other hand, only leads to small additional gains. However, a balanced combination of loosely coordinated basic controllers may be preferable.

These results indicate that DER could benefit from exploring the right balance of control in hybrid management systems, while efforts that focus only on perfecting control at a specific point or improving coordination between points may not produce cost effective solutions.

4   Conclusions

The energy market is a complex, intelligent, distributed system in a dynamic environment that needs to adapt continually, and thus needs to be designed to this purpose. The multi-agent systems and peer-to-peer paradigms together provide a promising frame of reference for the design of autonomic self-managed configurations of systems for the power grid.

Acknowledgments. This project is supported by the NLnet Foundation http://www.nlnet.nl. The authors thank Evangelos Pournaras for his contributions to this paper.

References

1. James, G., Peng, W., Deng, K.: Managing Household Wind-energy Generation. IEEE Intelligent Systems 23, 9–12 (2008)
2. Ogston, E., Zeman, A., Prokopenko, M., James, G.: Clustering Distributed Energy Resources for Large-Scale Demand Management. In: Proceedings of the 1st Int. Conf. Self-Adaptive and Self- Organizing Systems (SASO 2007), pp. 97–108. IEEE (2007)
3. Varga, L.Z., Jennings, N.R., Cockburn, D.: Integrating Intelligent Systems in to a Cooperating Community for Electricity Distribution Management. International Journal of Expert Systems with Applications 7, 563–579 (1994)
4. Jennings, N.R.: An agent-based approach for building complex software systems. Commun. ACM 44, 35–41 (2001)
5. Luis, M.: Complex system modeling: Using metaphors from nature in simulation and scientific methods. BITS: Computer and Communications News, Computing, Information and Communications Divisions (1999)
6. Theocharopoulou, C., Partsakoulakis, I., Vouros, G.A., Stergiou, K.: Overlay networks for task allocation and coordination in dynamic large-scale networks of co-operative agents. In: AAMAS 2007: Proceedings of the 6th International Joint Conference on Autonomous Agents and Multiagent Systems, pp. 1–8. ACM (2007)
7. A., J., Davidsson, P., Carlsson, B.: Coordination models for dynamic resource allocation. In: Coordination Models and Languages, pp. 182–197 (2000)
8. Mazza, P.: The smart energy network: Electrical power for the 21st century. Climate Solutions (2002)
9. Pournaras, E., Warnier, M., Brazier, F.M.T.: A distributed agent-based approach to stabilization of global resource utilization. In: The International Conference on Complex, Intelligent and Software Intensive Systems (CISIS 2009). IEEE (2009)
10. Hammerstrom, D.: Part II. Grid Friendly^{TM} Appliance Project. PNNL 17079, Pacific Northwestern National Laboratory (2002)
11. James, G., Cohen, D., Dodier, R., Platt, G., Palmer, D.: A deployed multi-agent framework for distributed energy applications. In: 5th International Joint Conference on Autonomous Agents and Multi-agent Systems (AAMAS 2006), Hakodate, Japan (2006)
12. Overeinder, B.J., Brazier, F.M.T.: Scalable Middleware Environment for Agent-Based Internet Applications. In: Dongarra, J., Madsen, K., Waśniewski, J. (eds.) PARA 2004. LNCS, vol. 3732, pp. 675–679. Springer, Heidelberg (2006)
13. Pournaras, E., Warnier, M., Brazier, F.M.T.: Adaptive Agent-based Self-organization for Robust Hierarchical Topologies. In: Proceedings of the First International Conference on Adaptive and Intelligent Systems (ICAIS 2009). IEEE (2009) (to appear)

14. Li, R., Wang, P.: Pattern Learning and Decision Making in a Photovoltaic System. In: Li, X., Kirley, M., Zhang, M., Green, D., Ciesielski, V., Abbass, H.A., Michalewicz, Z., Hendtlass, T., Deb, K., Tan, K.C., Branke, J., Shi, Y. (eds.) SEAL 2008. LNCS, vol. 5361, pp. 483–492. Springer, Heidelberg (2008)
15. Abu-Sharkh, S., Arnold, R., Kohler, J., Li, R., Markvart, T., Ross, J., Steemers, K., Wilson, P., Yao, R.: Can Microgrids Make a Major Contribution to UK Energy Supply? Renewable and Sustainable Energy Reviews 2, 78–127 (2006)
16. Hatziargyriou, N., Asano, H., Iravani, R., Marnay, C.: Microgrids. IEEE Power and Energy Magazine 4, 78–94 (2007)

Agent Roles for Context-Aware P2P Systems

Giacomo Cabri

Dipartimento di Ingegneria dell'Informazione,
Università di Modena e Reggio Emilia,
via Vignolese, 905,
41125 Modena, Italy
giacomo.cabri@unimore.it

Abstract. Roles represent a useful concept that has been successfully exploited to design and manage agent interactions in a context-aware fashion. For instance, they can be made available by a local context with specific features, or they can be exploited to enforce local policies while keeping general mechanisms. Moreover, one of the most important recognized advantage is that they allow a separation of concerns between algorithmic and interaction issues, simplifying the job of the developers of systems.

In this paper we propose to apply roles in the field of P2P systems, explaining which the related advantages and the issues to be faced are. We will also present an infrastructure, RoleX, which was conceived for agents' roles but can be adapted to P2P scenarios to accomplish this task.

1 Introduction

The *role* concept is effectively exploited in the agent world. A role defines a behavior that is common to different entities, so that systems can be analyzed, designed and implemented relying on such common behaviors without knowing details about the actual entities that will take part of the system. This is particularly useful in systems that exhibit a high degree of dynamism, and agent systems are a good example of such systems. In the literature we can find different proposals that exploit roles in the development of agent systems [13], covering different phases of the development, from analysis to implementation.

Peer-to-peer (P2P) systems can be considered very dynamic systems as well, since peers (nodes of a P2P network) cannot be classified as client or server in a static and definitive way [27], and often nodes can join and leave networks dynamically [5]. In addition, P2P systems that involve mobile devices must take into account also their mobility and the fact that the devices can can change "contexts" during their life [23].

In this scenario, this paper proposes to apply roles in the P2P field, in order to gain the same advantages that are recognized in the agent field.

The paper is organized as follows. First, we introduce the concept of role and the related advantages of exploiting it in modeling interactions (Section 2).

D. Beneventano et al. (Eds.): AP2PC 2008/2009, LNAI 6573, pp. 104–114, 2012.

Then, we explain how roles can be exploited in the P2P scenarios. To be concrete, we present also RoleX [10], an infrastructure developed inside the BRAIN framework [12]; it is reported as an example of infrastructure that can provide support for the management of roles (Section 4). Finally, before conclusions (Section 6), we report some related work in the field of role-based approaches for P2P and agents (Section 5).

2   Roles

Biddle and Thomas defined a *role* as "a set of *rights* and *duties*", in order to remark the twofold aspect of this concept [7]. Their work inspired the most of the role-based approaches, in particular those related to agents. In the following of this section we will focus on agents, but the same considerations can apply to entities in general, and to peers of P2P systems in particular.

Typically, a role is considered as a *stereotype of behavior* common to different agents in a given situation. Such a behavior is exhibited by the agent that plays the role, but is also expected by other entities, mainly other agents and organizations [24,33].

The role concept is useful in coordination, collaboration and in general in managing *interactions* between agents [9]. In fact, given the *sociality* feature of agents, roles are useful to model their interactions abstracting from the actual specific agents that will perform them; moreover, this concept is useful in the different phases of the agent system development.

There are different advantages in modeling interaction by roles and, consequently, in exploiting derived infrastructures. First, it enables a *separation of concerns* between the *algorithmic* issues and the *interaction* issues in developing agent-based applications, leaving the former to agents and the latter to roles. Second, it enables the *reuse of solutions and experiences*; in fact, roles are related to an application scenario, and designers can exploit roles previously defined for similar applications. In particular, roles can also be seen as sort of design patterns [2]: a set of related roles along with the definition of the way they interact can be considered as a solution to a well-defined problem, and reused in different similar situations.

3   Roles and P2P Systems

Even if roles have been mainly proposed in the agent field [13] and in the object-oriented programming [4], in this paper we propose to apply them also to the P2P field.

Note that we do not mean the traditional *client* and *server* "roles", which are not part of the nature of P2P systems. Instead, there could be a wide range of possible roles, depending also on the scenarios (see later an example of scenario). In addition, the capability of dynamically assuming roles can lead to more flexible solutions.

For instance, in an auction scenario, a peer can play the *bidder*, *seller* and *auctioneer* role. If the system is open, whatever peer can join, providing it can play the available roles. The auction context can be analyzed and designed considering roles, while the peers can be implemented focusing on bidding, buying and selling strategies, disregarding the interaction issue, which will be in charge of the assumed roles.

The *awareness* provided by this approach is related to the fact that the peers can have their strategies independent of local auction house, while the interaction mechanisms can have a local implementation while they are kept general from the peer's point of view. For instance, an auction house can decide to provide Web service to let peers interact, while others can rely on indirect communication such as tuple spaces [14]. But peers assume the same role and exploit the same functionalities, disregarding how they are implemented.

Besides mechanisms, roles can be exploited also to enforce local *policies*. In connection with the auction example, a site can decide to forbid interactions between bidders and sellers, to avoid collusion. This can be enacted by defining policies related to the roles, without knowing in advance which peer will play them.

Finally, when the implementation of roles must be updated, the developers can focus on them only, without needing to know which peers have played the roles in the past, nor which peers will play them in the future.

The mentioned advantages make roles interesting in the application to the P2P field, but of course also the issues of such an application must be considered; in our opinion, the major issue is related to deployment of roles, as explained in the next subsection.

3.1 Role Deployment

One of the most important issue to face in this context is the *role deployment*, i.e. the distribution of roles, no matter which their form is (from XML document to Java classes), in order to allow peers to assume, play and discard roles. To this purpose we sketch some solutions, proposed from the most static one to the most dynamic one.

The first solution is based on roles *hard coded* into the peers. Roles can be coded as "components" that can be linked directly from the peers' code. In this solution, the exploitation of roles can be useful to achieve part of the already sketched advantages, but when a peer must assume a new role, it must be re-coded. Such a recode work can be made easier if the *peer* logic and the *role* logic are clearly separated; this situation can happen if the interface between the different components is well-defined.

The second solution relies on peers that are *role providers*. In this solution, some peers of the system are in charge of keeping and providing roles to other peers. This makes this solution more dynamic than the previous one, since peers can decide to play a role at runtime, asking the needed role(s) to role providers without the need of recoding the peers themselves. Of course this introduces two main problems. First, the role providers can be considered as *servers*, which do not fit in the P2P way of conceiving distributed systems; second, a more philosophical issue is that the *role provider* can be a role itself. Nevertheless, this approach can enable peers to dynamically ask the *role provider* for interested role, and to assume them inside the network. Moreover, *hybrid networks* [27] in which some peer nodes provides given services, have been considered in the P2P world, so this solution can have some sense.

The third solution is based on the fact that each peer can have some initial roles, and then can *exchange* them with other peers, on the base of interest or need. In this way, there could be some kind of *epidemic* distribution of the roles. This can avoid the presence of specific role-provider peers in the network, but can make the search for appropriate roles more difficult. In fact, a peer that needs a specific role must search for it, for instance applying a neighborhood-based policy. This solution enforces context dependency, since neighbor peers are likely to have roles related to the local context where they are executing.

In general, Distributed Hash Tables (DHT) [3] can be exploited to share and retrieve the information about roles in a P2P network; then, once a suitable role is found, the peer can obtain the actual role (e.g., in the form of a component) following the second or the third above-mentioned solution. Otherwise, the DHT can directly provide the actual component that implements the role to the requesting peer. The former approach can involve negotiation between peers, useful if the management of roles requires also some sort of accounting. Of course, using DHT can decrease the context-awareness of a role-based approach, given their distributed nature; in this case, developers should evaluate the needed trade-off between availability of roles and their degree of connection to local contexts.

4 RoleX

RoleX is an example of infrastructure that can be exploited to provide support to the role management. It was initially thought for agents, but it can be adapted to support the P2P systems as well. In the following, with the term "agent" we mean an autonomous entity.

The BRAIN (Behavioural Roles for Agent INteractions) framework [1] proposes an approach where the interactions among agents are based on the concept of *role*. In the context of BRAIN, the RoleX (Role eXtension) interaction infrastructure has been implemented [8]. RoleX can easily associated to Java systems by adapting the few platform-dependent classes.

In RoleX, a role is defined as a set of *actions* that an agent playing such role can perform to achieve its task, and a set of *events* that an agent is expected to manage in order to "behave" as requested by the role it plays. Interactions between agents are then represented by couples *action-event*; in particular, an *action* of an agent A is translated into an *event* delivered to an agent B. So, on the one hand the interaction is determined by the role-available actions and events; on the other hand, such a translation can be performed and managed by the underlying interaction system, if present.

The meta-model of RoleX is reported in Figure 1, which shows the main entities of RoleX and their relationships.

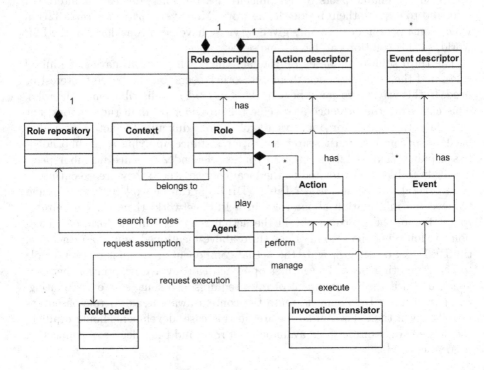

Fig. 1. RoleX meta-model

The management of roles in RoleX is highly dynamic, since an agent can assume at runtime roles even unknown at compile time, thanks to a special class loader called `RoleLoader`. Such a high dynamism is also granted by the exploitation of *descriptors*, which uncouple the physical implementation of a role (i.e., the Java class) from its features.

In RoleX, the fact that an agent assumes a role means that the infrastructure, via the already-mentioned `RoleLoader`, dynamically adds each role implementation member (both methods and fields) to agent members, in order to add the set of capabilities of the role, thus modifying and extending the agent class bytecode.

The sequence of activity performed in RoleX when an agent assumes roles and perform actions is reported in Figure 2.

When an agent wants to assume one or more roles to carry out its tasks, it queries the role repository in order to find the best role(s) for its needs. Then, the agent asks the `RoleLoader` to reload itself with the new role (or, better, with the role members added to the agent's one). This step can be repeated if the

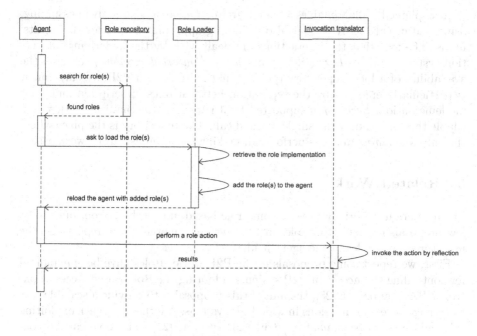

Fig. 2. RoleX sequence diagram

found roles are more than one. If everything is right, the `RoleLoader` sends the agent an event to indicate that the agent has been reloaded. After the reload event the agent can resume its execution.

The programmers do not know anything about the role implementation but know, by means of the descriptors, which actions can be used, and which events can occur. In the following, we focus on the action use, because the management of the events is similar and simpler. The use of descriptors means that the programmer cannot write code that invokes methods corresponding to role actions in the usual way, because a compile-time error will occur. Therefore, there must be an *invocation translator* that does introspection on the extended agent to dynamically find which method must be call in response to an invocation on an action description. When the agent invokes a role action, it specifies to the invocation translator a descriptor of the action that wants to perform, the translator searches for a method that corresponds to the description and then invokes it using the reflection.

To release a role, the process is similar to the addition, but this time the agent is reloaded without that role.

RoleX can be exploited to implement the part of the peer environment devoted to the role management, and the previously-introduced advantages can be concretely implemented by means of the RoleX features.

As explained, RoleX enables a high degree of *dynamisms* not only in assuming, using and discarding roles, but also in finding appropriate roles for the agents' needs. The fact that the interactions are dealt with by the underlying interaction system, enforces *local policies* and *rules*. *Context dependency* relies on the availability of a local repository (perhaps not suitable in a P2P system), but it is particularly enforced by the separation between roles' description and their implementation. *Security* is supported by JAAS-based mechanisms [11], which enable the control over the single method call. The repository is the place where the only role *maintenance* is performed, making the administrator's work easier.

5   Related Work

In this section we briefly present some role-based approaches. From our study, few proposals for exploiting roles in P2P systems emerge, so we report also the literature about roles in the agent field.

First, we report some proposals in the P2P world. Roles have been exploited for controlling the *access* in P2P systems, adopting the Role-Based Access Control (RBAC) approach [25]; the aim of this proposal is to provide a scalable way to manage access permissions in wide P2P systems. Another approach exploiting roles addresses *trust management* in P2P systems [21]; this topic can be considered similar to but of higher level than the access permission, and roles can simplify the management of trust. In [30], the authors give roles to the peers, but they are not considered as first-class entities, even if they are useful to classify the behavior of the peers in the network.

Much more proposals are present in the agent world. An interesting approach is AALAADIN [16], a meta-model to define models of organizations [17]. It is based on three core concepts: *agent*, *group* and *role*. Fasli's proposal is based on *social agents*, and joins several concepts, such as commitments and obligations, with the powerful of roles, promoting the use of a formal notation and analysis of the applications [15]. The GAIA [32] main aim is modelling multi-agent systems as *organizations* where different roles interact; GAIA exploits roles in particular in the *analysis* phase. E. Kendall well describes the importance of modeling roles for agent systems [20], and she proposes to exploit the Aspect Oriented Programming [22] to concretely implement the concept of role in agent applications. The Role/Interaction/Communicative Action (RICA) theory [28] was born with the main aim of improving the FIPA standard with support for social concepts, which are implemented in RICA-J. The Role based Evolutionary Programming (RoleEP) treats cooperative mobile agents, which belong to the same application and that collaborate to achieve a common goal [29]. The ROPE project [6] addresses the collaboration issues and recognizes the importance of defining roles as first-class entities, which can be assumed dynamically by agents. TRANS is a multi-agent system that provides for role and group behaviors, and takes into consideration mobile agents [18]; an interesting feature of TRANS is the capability of defining rules on the role assumption by agents, such as priority, exclusivity, compatibility and the distinction between permanent and temporary roles. The Tasks and Roles in a Unified Coordination Environment (TRUCE) is a script-based language framework for the coordination of agents [19], which aims to overtake problems related to *adaptability, heterogeneity* and *concurrency*. Yu and Schmid [31] exploit roles assigned to agents to manage workflow processes; they traditionally model a role as a collection of rights (activities an agent is permitted on a set of resources) and duties (activities an agent must perform); an interesting issue of this approach is that it aims to cover different phases of the application development, proposing a *role-based analysis phase*, an *agent-oriented design phase*, and an *agent-oriented implementation phase*. In [34] Zhu and Zhou describe a role model which is tied to both the computer and human parts involved in collaborations, and in particular tries to provide help to human in computer-supported collaborations.

6   Conclusion

In this paper we have proposed the adoption of the concept of *role* in the P2P field. The role concept has been widely exploited in the agent field, and our effort has been in the direction of showing that the advantages achieved in the agent field can be applied also to the P2P field.

The most relevant issue in P2P field is that we cannot rely on fixed infrastructure, so the management of the roles must be distributed among peers, differently from which happens for agents. In this paper we have sketched some possible solutions to exploit roles in P2P systems avoiding the presence of fixed infrastructures, and adapting existing infrastructures such as RoleX.

With regard to future work, we are evaluating the chance of building methodologies that focus on roles [26] and are suitable for a variety of scenarios; among others, the P2P scenario is one good candidate for our evaluation. In addition, it is worth studying the proposal of P2P architectures that enable the management of roles in a distributed way, following the directions sketched in this paper; the appropriate exploitation of DHT is worth studying to evaluate their involvement in some of the proposed directions. Putting all together, an interesting research direction is to study how to connect the *concept* of role managed in the methodologies with the *implementation* of role provided by infrastructures, in order to avoid fragmented solutions.

Acknowledgements. Work supported by the Italian MiUR in the frame of the PRIN project "MEnSA - Agent oriented methodologies: engineering of interactions and relationship with the infrastructures".

References

1. The AgentGroup. The BRAIN framework (2007),
   http://www.agentgroup.unimo.it/MOON/BRAIN
2. Aridor, Y., Lange, D.: Agent Design Pattern: Elements of Agent Application design. In: Proceedings of the International Conference on Autonomous Agents. ACM Press (1998)
3. Balakrishnan, H., Kaashoek, M.F., Karger, D., Morris, R., Stoica, I.: Looking up data in P2P systems. Communications of the ACM 46(2), 43–48 (2003)
4. Bäumer, D., Riehle, D., Siberski, W., Wulf, M.: The role object pattern. Washington University Dept. of Computer Science (1997)
5. Bawa, M., Gionis, A., Garcia-Molina, H., Motwani, R.: The price of validity in dynamic networks. Journal of Computer and System Sciences 73(3), 245–264 (2007)
6. Becht, M., Gurzki, T., Klarmann, J., Muscholl, M.: ROPE: Role Oriented Programming Environment for Multiagent Systems. In: Proceedings of the Fourth IFCIS Conference on Cooperative Information Systems (CoopIS 1999), Edinburgh, Scotland (1999)
7. Biddle, B.J., Thomas, E.J.: Role Theory: Concepts and Research. R. E. Krieger Publishing Co. (1979)
8. Cabri, G., Ferrari, L., Leonardi, L.: Enabling mobile agents to dynamically assume roles. In: Proceedings of the 2003 ACM International Symposium on Applied Computing (SAC). ACM, Melbourne (2003)
9. Cabri, G., Ferrari, L., Leonardi, L.: Agent role-based collaboration and coordination: a survey about existing approaches. In: Proceedings of the 2004 IEEE International Conference on Systems, Man and Cybernetics, The Hague, Netherlands (2004)
10. Cabri, G., Ferrari, L., Leonardi, L.: The RoleX Environment for Multi-agent Cooperation. In: Klusch, M., Ossowski, S., Kashyap, V., Unland, R. (eds.) CIA 2004. LNCS (LNAI), vol. 3191, pp. 257–270. Springer, Heidelberg (2004)
11. Cabri, G., Ferrari, L., Leonardi, L.: Applying Security Policies Through Agent Roles: a JAAS Based Approach. Science of Computer Programming 59(1-2), 127–146 (2006)
12. Cabri, G., Leonardi, L., Zambonelli, F.: BRAIN: A Framework for Flexible Role-Based Interactions in Multiagent Systems. In: Meersman, R., Schmidt, D.C. (eds.) CoopIS 2003, DOA 2003, and ODBASE 2003. LNCS, vol. 2888, pp. 145–161. Springer, Heidelberg (2003)
13. Cabri, G., Ferrari, L., Leonardi, L., Zambonelli, F.: A Survey about Role-based Interaction Proposals for Agents. Technical Report Technical report DII-AG-2005-1, Dipartimento di Ingegneria dell'Informazione (2005)
14. Cabri, G., Leonardi, L., Zambonelli, F.: Auctio-Based Agent Negotiation via Programmable Tuple Spaces. In: Klusch, M., Kerschberg, L. (eds.) CIA 2000. LNCS (LNAI), vol. 1860, pp. 83–94. Springer, Heidelberg (2000)
15. Fasli, M.: Social Interactions in Multi-Agent Systems: A Formal Approach. In: Proceedings of the IEEE/WIC International Conference on Intelligent Agent Technology (IAT 2003), pp. 240–247. IEEE Press (2003)
16. Ferber, J., Gutknecht, O.: AALAADIN: A meta-model for the analysis and design of organizations in multi-agent systems. In: Proceedings of the Third International Conference on Multi-Agent Systems, ICMAS 1998 (1998)

17. Ferber, J., Gutknecht, O., Michel, F.: From Agents to Organizations: An Organizational View of Multi-agent Systems. In: Giorgini, P., Müller, J.P., Odell, J.J. (eds.) AOSE 2003. LNCS, vol. 2935, pp. 214–230. Springer, Heidelberg (2004)

18. Fournier, S., Brocarei, D., Devogele, T., Claramunt, C.: TRANS: A Tractable Role-based Agent Prototype for Concurrent Navigation Systems. In: Proceedings of the First European Workshop on Multi-Agent Systems (EUMAS), Oxford, UK (2003)

19. Jamison, W.C., Lea, D.: TRUCE: Agent Coordination through Concurrent Interpretation of Role-Based Protocols. In: Ciancarini, P., Wolf, A.L. (eds.) COORDINATION 1999. LNCS, vol. 1594, pp. 384–398. Springer, Heidelberg (1999)

20. Kendall, E.A.: Role Modelling for Agent Systems Analysis, Design and Implementation. IEEE Concurrency 8(2), 34–41 (2000)

21. Khambatti, M., Dasgupta, P., Ryu, K.D.: A role-based trust model for peer-to-peer communities and dynamic coalitions. In: Proceedings of the Second IEEE International Information Assurance Workshop, vol. 154 (2004)

22. Kiczales, G., Lamping, J., Mendhekar, A., Maeda, C., Lopes, C., Loingtier, J.M., Irwin, J.: Aspect-Oriented Programming. Technical report, Xerox Corporation (1997)

23. Kortuem, G., Schneider, J., Preuitt, D., Thompson, T.G.C., Fickas, S., Segall, Z.: When peer-to-peer comes face-to-face: Collaborative peer-to-peer computing in mobile ad hoc networks. In: Proceedings of the First International Conference on Peer-to-Peer Computing (P2P 2001). IEEE Computer Society (2001)

24. Odell, J.J., Parunak, H.V.D., Fleischer, M.: The Role of Roles in Designing Effective Agent Organizations. In: Garcia, A., et al. (eds.) SELMAS 2002. LNCS, vol. 2603, pp. 27–38. Springer, Heidelberg (2003)

25. Park, J.S., Hwang, J.: Role-based access control for collaborative enterprise in peer-to-peer computing environments. In: Proceedings of the Eighth ACM Symposium on Access Control Models and Technologies, pp. 93–99. ACM, New York (2003)

26. Puviani, M., Cabri, G., Leonardi, L.: Agent Roles: from Methodologies to Infrastructures. In: The 2008 Workshop on Role-Based Collaboration, at the 2008 International Symposium on Collaborative Technologies and Systems (CTS 2008), Irvine California, USA (May 2008)

27. Schollmeier, R.: A definition of peer-to-peer networking for the classification of peer-to-peer architectures and applications. In: Peer-to-Peer Computing, pp. 101–102 (2001)

28. Serrano, J.M., Ossowski, S.: On the Impact of Agent Communication Languages on the Implementation of Agent Systems. In: Klusch, M., Ossowski, S., Kashyap, V., Unland, R. (eds.) CIA 2004. LNCS (LNAI), vol. 3191, pp. 92–106. Springer, Heidelberg (2004)

29. Ubayashi, N., Tamai, T.: RoleEP: role based evolutionary programming for cooperative mobile agent applications. In: Proceedings of the International Symposium on Principles of Software Evolution, Kanazawa, Japan (2000)

30. Verma, K., Sivashanmugam, K., Sheth, A., Patil, A., Oundhakar, S., Miller, J.: Meteor-s wsdi: A scalable p2p infrastructure of registries for semantic publication and discovery of web services. Information Technology and Management 6(1), 17–39 (2005)

31. Yu, L., Schmid, B.F.: A conceptual framework for agent-oriented and role-based workflow modelling. In: Proceedings of the 1st International Workshop on Agent-Oriented Information Systems (1999)

32. Zambonelli, F., Jennings, N., Wooldridge, M.: Developing Multiagent Systems: the Gaia Methodology. ACM Transactions on Software Engineering and Methodology 12(3) (2003)
33. Zambonelli, F., Jennings, N.R., Wooldridge, M.: Organizational Rules as an Abstraction for the Analysis and Design of Multi-agent Systems. International Journal of Software Engineering and Knowledge Engineering 11(3), 303–328 (2001)
34. Zhu, H., Zhou, M.C.: Role-Based Collaborations and their Kernel Mechanisms. IEEE Transactions. on Systems, Man and Cybernetics, Part C 36(4), 578–589 (2006)

Working in a Dynamic Environment:
The NeP4B Approach as a MAS⋆

Sonia Bergamaschi[1], Francesco Guerra[2],
Federica Mandreoli[1,3], and Maurizio Vincini[1]

[1] DII-Università di Modena e Reggio Emilia
via Vignolese 905, 41100 Modena
firstname.lastname@unimore.it
[2] DEA-Università di Modena e Reggio Emilia
v.le Berengario 51, 41100 Modena
[3] IEIIT-BO/CNR
viale Risorgimento, 2, 40132 Bologna
firstname.lastname@unimore.it

Abstract. Integration of heterogeneous information in the context of
Internet is becoming a key activity to enable a more organized and semantically meaningful access to several kinds of information in the form
of data sources, multimedia documents and web services. In NeP4B (Networked Peers for Business), a project funded by the Italian Ministry of
University and Research, we developed an approach for providing a uniform representation of data, multimedia and services, thus allowing users
to obtain sets of data, multimedia documents and lists of webservices as
query results. NeP4B is based on a P2P network of semantic peers, connected one with each other by means of automatically generated mappings. In this paper we present a new architecture for NeP4B, based on
a Multi-Agent System. We claim that such a solution may be more efficient and effective, thanks to the agents autonomy and intelligence, in
a dynamic environment, where sources are frequently added (or deleted)
to (from) the network.

1   Introduction

The computer science technology has been developing different techniques for
representing, managing and retrieving information. Recently, Internet is defi-
nitely becoming one of the most relevant repositories where finding information
about several topics. Managing information sources on Internet implies to address big challenging issues mainly related to: 1) the management of their heavy
heterogeneity, and 2) the autonomy of the sources that change their contents
and structures without any notification and independently of the other sources.

In the last decades, the research community has been investigating about the
management of the heterogeneity of the sources. Techniques for reconciliating different representations of the same real world objects in terms of granularities and

---

⋆ This work was partially supported by MUR co-funded project NeP4B
(http://www.dbgroup.unimo.it/nep4b).

D. Beneventano et al. (Eds.): AP2PC 2008/2009, LNAI 6573, pp. 115–128, 2012.
© Springer-Verlag Berlin Heidelberg 2012

structures have been developed [25]. We claim that a different kind of heterogeneity has not been until now investigated concerning the different kinds of media that may be adopted for conveying information. With reference to Internet, we may consider: data sources (that are roughly categorized in structured sources as databases, semi-structured as XML and RDF/OWL files and unstructured as the HTML documents); web-services that are exploited for managing data using a pre-fixed interface and multimedia documents (images, audio and video files).

From the user perspective, data, multimedia documents and services provide a complementary vision of the domain they refer to: data provides detailed information about precise aspects, a multimedia file may be considered as a special data-type used for describing an instance, services make software components and business applications available via standardized interfaces. By now, the research about data, multimedia, and services has involved different, not always overlapped communities. It is over 20 years that the research community has been developing techniques for integrating heterogeneous data sources. The recent progress on the description and discovery of semantic Web services has made available modular, self-describing and self-contained applications over the Internet. Similarity search for content-based retrieval (where contents can be any combination of text, image, audio/video, etc.) has gained more and more importance in recent years, also because of the advantage of ranking the retrieved results according to their proximity to a query. Thus these three kinds of sources adopt different data and search models, and are usually exploited by different users categories, having different querying requirements.

The current research on querying integrated data sources, multimedia and web services discovering is no longer enough for the actual users requirements. A new research perspective, where data and services are considered as complementary views of the same domain and consequently managed with the same tools, is needed. In the NeP4B project we propose an approach for dealing with these different information sources through a common framework. The NeP4B approach builds a P2P network of information sources (data, multimedia and services) grouped in semantic peers. Each semantic peer is data-centric, i.e. it builds a unified view of data sources in the form of a Single Peer Data Ontology (SPDO) representing both traditional and multimedia sources. By means of mappings, the ontologies used for modeling web services and data are linked, thus creating a Peer Virtual View (PVV) and such connections are exploited for answering queries about data with a set of related services.

In this paper we present a new architecture for NeP4B, based on a Multi-Agent System. We claim that such a solution may be more efficient and effective, thanks to the agents autonomy and intelligence, in a dynamic environment, where sources are frequently added (or deleted) to (from) the network. The proposed MAS is made up of several semantic peer agents that, independently, carry out data and service searches and exchange knowledge with other peers. Each semantic peer includes list of neighbor peers with mappings between the the semantic peer and the other in the network. Such knowledge allows to propagate a query a user formulate according to a Semantic Peer into a set of queries to be executed by the other peers in the network. Two other kinds of agent complete the network: the Access Point Agent that manages the networks noticing when a new peer is accepted or removed from the network and the User Agent created for managing the query execution, propagation and the results collection.

This paper is organized as follows: next section overviews the NeP4B approach; section 3 introduces the main kinds of implemented agents; section 4 introduces some related work and finally section 5 sketches out some conclusions and future work.

2   The NeP4B Approach

In NeP4B, data sources, multimedia sources and services are grouped into semantic peers. Each semantic peer generates a Peer Virtual View (PVV), i.e. a unified representation of the data, multimedia and the services held by the sources belonging to the peer. A PVV is made up of the following components, shown in Figure 1:

- a **Semantic Peer Data Ontology (SPDO)** of traditional and multimedia data, i.e. a common representation of all the data sources belonging to the peer built by exploiting a properly extended mediator based system.
- a **Global Light Service Ontology (GLSO)** that provides, by means of a set of concepts and attributes, a global view of all the concepts and attributes viewed for the descriptions of the Web services available in the peer. Information Retrieval techniques are exploited for transforming an SQL query over the SPDO into a keyword based search on the GLSO;
- a set of **mappings**, automatically computed, which connects GLSO elements to SPDO elements.

The processes for creating and querying the PVV are sketched out in next sections. More details are shown in [5,24].

Semantic peers behave as independent and interoperable nodes of a virtual peer-to- peer (P2P) network for data and service sharing. The proposed infrastructure is briefly presented in section 2.3 while more details can be found in [19,14,20,17].

2.1   Creating the PVV

The approach for building the PVV consists of three processes: the SPDO and the GLSO creation, which are independent processes and the generation of mappings between the elements of the two ontologies.

Creating the SPDO. The SPDO, i.e. a conceptualizations of a set of data and multimedia sources, is composed of global classes and attributes and mappings between the SPDO and the local source schemata. The SPDO is built by coupling and extending the two previously developed MOMIS and MILOS

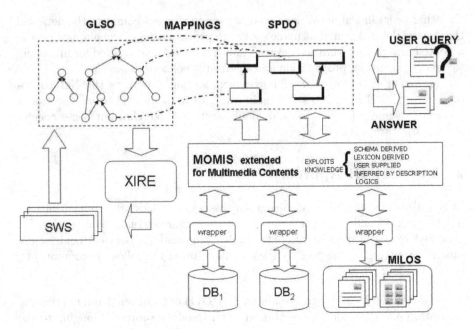

Fig. 1. The NeP4B PVV

systems. MOMIS (Mediator environment for Multiple Information Sources)[1] [6] is a framework to perform integration of structured and semi-structured data sources, plus a query management environment able to process incoming queries on the integrated schema. MILOS [1] is a Multimedia Content Management System tailored to support design and implementation of digital library applications. MILOS supports the storage and content based retrieval of any multimedia document whose description is provided by using arbitrary metadata models represented in XML. The process is based on three functional steps based on an extensions of MOMIS:

1. by means of wrappers, descriptions of traditional data source schemata are translated in a common language (ODLI3, an extension of the standard ODL-ODMG). MILOS is exploited as a wrapper for multimedia sources.
2. source descriptions are analyzed and a CommonThesaurus of structural and lexical derived relationships plus relationships provided by the user is built. Moreover the Common Thesaurus is enriched with automatically inferred relationships with Description Logics techniques.
3. a clustering technique applied to the source descriptions and exploiting the relationships in the Common Thesaurus, allows MOMIS to generate a set of global classes which are representative of the involved sources. For each global class, a mapping table represents the mappings between the local classes and the global class.

---

[1] http://www.dbgroup.unimo.it/Momis for publications about MOMIS.

Creating the GLSO. The GLSO is built by means of a process, applied to the Service Ontologies (SO) which the web services refer to, consisting of three main steps: (i) service indexing, (ii) Global Service Ontology (GSO) construction, (iii) Global Light Service Ontology (GLSO) construction and Semantic Similarity Matrix (SSM) definition:

1. Service Indexing: in order to inquiry services, an Information Retrieval (IR) approach applied to semantic descriptions of Web services has been developed. In particular, we consider each service as a structured document and an inverted index, where service name, service description, input, output, pre-condition and postcondition are described.
2. The SOs are merged, by a loosely merging process which automatically integrates similar concepts, thus creating a Global Service Ontology (GSO).
3. Since the GSO may result extremely large in size, a technique to reduce the ontology size is exploited and the GLSO is obtained. A Semantic Similarity Matrix representing the semantic similarity between two terms in the GLSO is finally built.

Generation of Mappings. Mappings between the elements of the SPDO and the GLSO are generated by exploiting and properly modifying the MOMIS clustering algorithm. The clustering algorithm takes as input the SPDO and the GLSO with their associated metadata and generates a set of clusters of classes belonging to the SPDO and the GLSO. On the basis of the cluster composition, mappings connecting SPDO and GLSO elements are automatically generated.

2.2 Querying the PVV

NeP4B follows a data-centric approach: a query over an SPDO returns data satisfying the query constraints and services related to the query elements. Query processing is thus divided into two steps, that are simultaneously executed:

– a data set from the data sources is obtained with query processing on an integrated view;
– a set of services related to the query is obtained by exploiting the mappings between SPDO and GLSO.

Data results are obtained by exploiting the MOMIS Query Manager (see [3] for a complete description) which rewrites the global query as an equivalent set of queries expressed on the local schemata (local queries); this query translation is carried out by considering the mappings between the SPDO and the local schemata. Since MOMIS follows a GAV approach, this mapping is expressed by specifying, for each global class C, a mapping query QC over the schemata of the local classes belonging to C. The query translation is thus performed by means of query unfolding. Results from the local sources are then merged exploiting the reconciliation techniques. Query processing is more complex than in traditional data integration systems as multimedia data are considered [5].

Services are retrieved by the XIRE (eXtended Information Retrieval Engine) component, which is a service search engine based on the vector space model [8]; in particular, the approach uses a vector where each term has a relevance weight associated. The vector is built by 1) extracting the SPDO terms appearing in the data query; 2) exploiting the mappings for identifying the GLSO elements that are mapped on those SPDO terms.

2.3   The Network of Semantic Peers

Semantic peers interoperate for data and service sharing purposes through a P2P architecture where pairs or small groups of peers are locally connected through mappings which are established among their PVVs. Semantic mappings are exploited for query processing purpose: in order to query a peer, its own SPDO is used for query formulation and semantic mappings are used to reformulate the query over its immediate neighbors, then over their immediate neighbors, and so on, following a semantic path of mappings. In this respect, the main role of mappings is to overcome the absence of a common understanding of the vocabularies used at each peers schema, thus implementing a decentralized schema mediation. For this reason, each mapping is appropriately extended with a score which gives a measure of the semantic compatibility occurring between involved concepts.

In the NeP4B project, we developed a (semi)automatic tool which receives in input a pair of SPDOs and provides a set of plausible mappings defining how to represent the source schema in terms of the destination schema vocabulary. The proposed matching algorithm [13] essentially exploits the schema property semantics to infer new properties, assigns an initial semantic similarity score between each pair of concepts in the two schemas, and adopts the similarity flooding approach proposed in [22], where schemas are treated as directed labeled graphs and used in an iterative fixpoint computation whose results tell us what nodes in one graph are similar to nodes in the second graph. Starting from this intermediate result, besides class-to-class matching and property-to-property matches, the proposed algorithm is also able to derive property-to- path matches by combining a label similarity approach with a learning approach which exploits user feedback in order to promote the most plausible matches.

3   The NeP4B Agents at Work

The approach aims at building a completely decentralized Multi-Agent Data and Service System, i.e. mediator-free system for P2P network [28], by introducing an architecture without a centralized information mediator system. The agent network is built by means of a semi-automatic process and consists of several kinds of agents, *the User Agent (UA), Semantic Peer Agent (SPA), Query Agent (QA) and Access Point Agent (APA)* with specific roles and behaviors implemented in the network (see figure 2). From a deployment perspective, the NeP4B network has been developed by using the Java Agent DEvelopment (JADE) platform[2].

---

[2] http://jade.tilab.com/

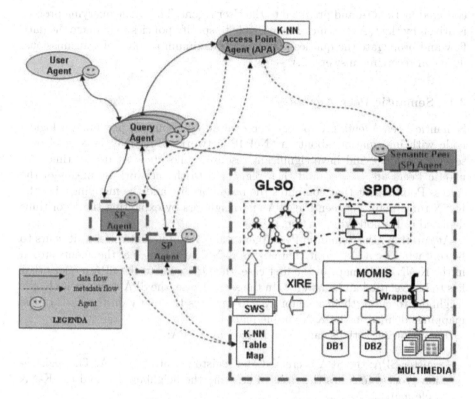

Fig. 2. The NeP4B Agents at work

The first step towards a unified view of data, multimedia and services is the building of a PVV of the information sources composing the Semantic Peer. Semantic Peers expose their PVVs by means of Semantic Peer Agents. Moreover, some other information about the networks of peers are collected by the SPAs, i.e. the list of the closest peers and mappings among the main concepts in the near peers according to the technique depicted in fig. 2.3. The list of closest peers is exploited for propagating a query that a user formulates according to PVV.

A Semantic Peer becomes part of the NeP4B Network by means of its registration into the Access Point Agent (APA) which is unique in the network. The APA accepts (or refuses) the registration according with specific (business) rules implemented by the network manager. When a new SPA is accepted in the network, the APA computes the semantically close peers and the mappings between the SPA and the retrieved peers. Such information is stored by the new SPA.

A User Agent encapsulates the end users requests, which is formulated by expressing constraints on the PVV elements (classes and properties) of a specific SPA. After the query composition, a Query Agent is generated. On the basis of the SPA mappings, the QA transforms each query into a set of queries to be executed by the near peers. An SPA involved by a rewritten query may propagate the query to other peers following the same mechanism. The results are then collected by the QA and provided to the User Agent. The whole querying process is driven by the QA for which it is possible to specify policies to manage the data flow and propagate the queries (in terms of maximum number of transmissions, delays in receiving answers, ...).

3.1 Semantic Peer Agents

Semantic Peer Agents group together several data sources, providing a logical node with information about the NeP4B network. SPAs may be spread over several machines and have significant resources allocated. At design time, Semantic Peers are created and then registered to the network by means of the Access Point Agent that computes the neighbors list and the mappings, i.e. the K-NN table map, between the SPA and neighbors by exploiting the algorithms depicted in the following section.

At run time, the Semantic Peer Agent plays two different roles: a) it waits to be contacted by a QA; b) it contacts its K-NN neighbors, i.e. the agents stored in the K-NN table map. In the first case, the QA sends to the SPA a query that has to be executed and answered. In the second case, the SPA contacts its K-NN neighbors to check their availability and rewrites the query on the basis of the mappings defined in the K-NN table map.

The following actions can be performed by a SPA:

- register-SPA: the SPA is created and registered into the APA. The registration process includes the tasks of creating the neighbors list and the K-NN table map;
- process-query: the query sent by a QA is executed according to the PVV and the results (data and services) are sent to the QA;
- reformulate-query: the query sent by a QA is reformulated on the basis of the K-NN table map into a set of queries to be executed by the neighbors SPA.

3.2 Access Point Agent

The Access Point Agent role is to accept or refuse a new SPA in the network. In our approach there is only one APA in the network. If a new SPA is accepted in the network, the list of neighbors agents and the mappings between the new SPA and the network are computed. Moreover, an APA is in charge of managing the removal of a SPA from the network. In this case, all the SPAs having the SPA to be removed in their neighbors list and K-NN table map, have to be updated.

Therefore, the following actions can be performed by an APA:

- register-SPA: the conditions for the acceptance of a newly entering SPA are checked and the K-NN SPAs are computed;
- compute-mapping: the mappings between a pair of SPAs are computed by means of the algorithm described in Sec. 2 and communicated to the involved SPAs;
- remove-SPA: all the SPAs neighbors are informed of the SPA exiting.

As far as the network organization is involved, the main aim of the APA is to efficiently support the creation and maintenance of a scalable network that clusters
together heterogeneous peers which are semantically related. To this end, the
network is organized in a set of Semantic Overlay Networks (SONs) [10] where
each SON is a group of semantically related nodes locally connected through a
link structure. Newly entering SPAs are assigned to one or more SONs on the
basis of their own topics of interest. To this extent, the APA maintains a light
structure, the Access Point Structure (APS) [17], which provides cumulative
information about each SON available in the network such as the SONs representative concepts, which the peer compares with its concepts, and the SON
clustroid which is an SPA. The latter is then used by the APA to start navigat-
ing the link structure within each selected SON with the aim of searching for
the K-NN SPAs. Once they have been selected, the APA computes the mapping
between the PVV of the newly entering SPA and each neighbor.

3.3   User Agents

User Agents are in charge of all the search activities in the NeP4B network,
having mainly a coordination role. The main functions implemented in a UA
are:

- browse network: by means of this function a user may browse the SPA network and select the SPA of interest on the basis of its PVV.
- get-PVV: the PVV of an SPA is shown to the user in order to allow the
  query formulation;
- create-query: queries are formulated in SPARQL-like language (by means of
  the user interface) properly extended to support similarity predicates on the
  multimedia data [12];
- process-query: when the user finished the query creation, two tasks are accomplished: a new QA is created, and the query translated into the internal
  query language is passed within a message to the QA.
- receive-results: by means of this function, the results collected by a QA are
  received and shown to the user.

3.4   Query Agent

The Query Agents goal is to define and execute the query process. This task is
performed by means of two different processes involving the initial SPA:

1. the QA translates the SPARQL query into the internal language and obtain
   the list of SPAs to be inquired;
2. starting from the queried peer, the query is first reformulated over its immediate neighbors, then over their neighbors, and so on.

Query spreading is thus a fundamental task, since the ability to obtain relevant
data from other nodes in a network depends on the existence of a semantic path
of mappings from the queried peer to that node [27].

Starting from our past experiences on semantic query routing [19,21], we propose to combine this kind of routing with a multimedia routing approach [15] in order to devise an innovative mechanism which exploits the two main aspects characterizing the querying process in such a context: the semantics of the concepts in the peers PVVs and the multimedia contents in the peers repositories. More precisely, since the reformulation process may lead to some semantic approximation, we pursue effectiveness by selecting, for each query, the peers which are semantically best suited for answering it. We quantify the semantic approximation due to a one-step reformulation in accordance with the semantic mapping scores and composes semantic approximation scores to deal with multi-step reformulations. Intuitively, the higher the score the more relevant the returned answers. Therefore, we make the user aware of the relevance of the answers gathered through the network by means of a ranking mechanism which promotes the most semantically related results.

The life cycle of a QA is initiated by an invocation of solve-query service, and it is finished when results are delivered. The following actions are combined in a QA to respond to a solve-query demand:

- validate-query: The agent must parse the query received from the UA in order to check whether it is well-defined, and to extract from it the information about the initial SPA.
- query-expansion-SPA: This action translates the query in terms of the SPA PVV, and into a set of relevant queries related to the near SPAs.
- query-SP: By means this action, the Semantic Peers useful to answer the query are contacted. Since the adopted algorithm guarantees that the queries are executed in a relevance order, the results are shown to the user as soon as they are received.
- deliver-result: When the query process is finished, the results are returned to the UA by means of this action.

4   Related Work

Several agent-based information retrieval systems have been developed. Some of the ideas used for making agents the NeP4B project may be compared with Sewasie[3] a research project, we participated in, funded by the European Commission, aimed to design and implement an advanced search engine enabling intelligent access to heterogeneous data sources on the web via semantic enrichment to provide the basis of structured secure web-based communication. IN SEWASIE strongly tied local nodes are integrated into semantic peers and Mediator Agents provide globally integrated ontologies by means of mappings [4]. Differently from this approach, we developed a mediator-free multi-agent data integration system, where an Access Point Agent collects the list of agents in the network and each peer has information about the neighbors ones. The overall architecture may be compared also with the one proposed in [28], that differs

---

[3] http://www.sewasie.org

from our approach with respect to the semantic peer structure and the algorithm for retrieving, distributing and rewriting queries in the network.

Other multi agent system have been developed for addressing data integration issues. CARROT II [9] is one of the most well-known systems: it is an agent-based architecture for distributed information retrieval and document collection management. It consists of an arbitrary number of agents providing search services over local document collections or information sources. They contain meta-data describing their local documents which are sent to other agents that act as brokers. In [7] an approach for complex data integration that uses both classical warehousing approach and multi-agents systems technology is proposed. Knowledge bases have been managed by means of MAS: in [26] a framework for knowledge discovery, knowledge use, and knowledge management to provide knowledge-based access of the domain databases is presented. This framework encompasses five different agents: namely, knowledge management agent, data filter agent, rule induction agent, dynamic analysis agent, and interface agent. Concerning the Semantic Peer Agent, we may compare our work with [18] introducing a mediator system based on agents for generating and maintaining the data. Differently from this approach, we rely on wrappers (and not on agents) for updating the data and the mediator is based on lexical, structural knowledge for building a unified view.

Several surveys about the approaches in the ontology management area have been published. This topic is generally divided into three categories: ontology development, ontology and schema matching and ontology alignment. Concerning the ontology development, the ONTOWEB project published a complete technical report (http://www.ontoweb.org deliverable 1.4) where tools are classified on the basis of the implemented methodologies (from scratch, reengineering ontologies, based on a cooperative construction, and managing the evolution). Several researchers address topics in the ontology matching area, i.e. the techniques for identifying similar concepts in different ontologies: in several systems are evaluated on the basis of the generated mappings [25] (five kinds of criteria are identified), while [23] focuses on mapping discovery, reasoning and representation. The ontology alignment, i.e. the automated resolution of semantic correspondences between the elements of heterogeneous ontologies, is one of the new challenge in the ontology management and it includes ontology mapping and schema mapping. The Knowledgeweb Network of Excellence (http://knowledgeweb.semanticweb.org) has largely investigated about this issue publishing several reports. In the following paragraphs, we shall compare some ontology management system with our approach. Clio [16] is a research prototype providing to the user a graphical interface in order to support the creation of mappings between two data representations. There are many differences between Clio and our data integration system: first, in the Clio framework the focus is on schema mapping issues, while the focus of our proposal is the semiautomatic generation of a target schema common to each source (the Global Virtual View). Moreover, our proposal relies on structural and lexical relationships between the sources. COMA++ [2] is a composite matcher which provides an extensible library of different matchers and supports various aggregating and selecting strategies. Matchers exploit linguistic, data-type, and structural information, as well as previous matches, to produce similarity matrices. Particular similarity values are then selected as suitable match candidates, and combined into a single value. This process is performed for whole schemata or for two schema elements, and is repeated after the user provides feedback. COMA supports a reuse approach focusing on existing mappings, which can be generalized for different reuse granularities, or fragment- and schema-level match results. The starting mappings (or similarity) are user-defined, unlike our approach that is mainly focused on the use of lexical dictionaries (like WordNet) to discover semantic relationships. GLUE and iMAP [11] aim to semi-automatically find schema mappings for data integration. Like its ancestor LSD, Glue uses machine learning techniques to find mappings [11]. It first applies statistical analysis to the available data (joint probability distribution computation). It then generates a similarity matrix, based on the probability distributions, for the data considered and uses constraint relaxation in order to obtain an alignment from the similarity, which is obtained by using probabilistic definition of several similarity measures. This approach relies on data instances techniques. On the other hand, the our methodology is based on schema analysis.

5   Conclusion and Future Work

In this paper, a multi agent system for supporting the query execution in a distributed environment is proposed.

The network has been experimented in the NeP4B project, where Enterprises create a knowledge network for providing information about their activities and looking for supports from other companies. This is a dynamic environment, since new enterprises may join or leave the network with frequent changes. We think that in such an environment, an agent architecture may really provide a useful coordination support.

Future work will be addressed to complete the implementation and the testing of the network and to the experimentation of the system in a real scenario.

References

1. Amato, G., Gennaro, C., Rabitti, F., Savino, P.: Milos: A Multimedia Content Management System for Digital Library Applications. In: Heery, R., Lyon, L. (eds.) ECDL 2004. LNCS, vol. 3232, pp. 14–25. Springer, Heidelberg (2004)
2. Aumueller, D., Do, H.H., Massmann, S., Rahm, E.: Schema and ontology matching with coma++. In: Ozcan, F. (ed.) SIGMOD Conference, pp. 906–908. ACM (2005)
3. Beneventano, D., Bergamaschi, S.: Semantic Search Engines based on Data Integration Systems. In: Cardoso, J. (ed.) Semantic Web: Theory, Tools and Applications. Idea Group Publishing (forthcoming), http://www.dbgroup.unimo.it
4. Beneventano, D., Bergamaschi, S., Guerra, F., Vincini, M.: The sewasie network of medi-ator agents for semantic search. J. UCS 13(12), 1936–1969 (2007)

5. Beneventano, D., Gennaro, C., Guerra, F.: A methodology for building and querying an ontology representing data and multimedia sources. In: ODBIS, pp. 37–40 (2008)

6. Bergamaschi, S., Castano, S., Beneventano, D., Vincini, M.: Semantic integration of heterogenous information sources. Journal of Data and Knowledge Engineering 36(3), 215–249 (2001)

7. Boussaid, O., Bentayeb, F., Darmont, J.: An mas-based etl approach for complex data. CoRR, abs/0809.2686 (2008)

8. Christopher, P.R., Manning, D., Schutze, H.: Introduction to Information Retrieval. Cambridge University Press (2008)

9. Cost, R.S., Kallurkar, S., Majithia, H., Nicholas, C., Shi, Y.: Integrating Distributed Information Sources with CARROT II. In: Klusch, M., Ossowski, S., Shehory, O. (eds.) CIA 2002. LNCS (LNAI), vol. 2446, pp. 194–201. Springer, Heidelberg (2002)

10. Crespo, A., Garcia-Molina, H.: Semantic Overlay Networks for P2P Systems. In: Moro, G., Bergamaschi, S., Aberer, K. (eds.) AP2PC 2004. LNCS (LNAI), vol. 3601, pp. 1–13. Springer, Heidelberg (2005)

11. Doan, A., Madhavan, J., Domingos, P., Halevy, A.Y.: Learning to map between ontologies on the semantic web. In: WWW, pp. 662–673 (2002)

12. Gennaro, C., Lenzi, R., Mandreoli, F., Martoglia, R., Mordacchini, M.: Design of procedures and structures for the support of the inter-peer semantic queries. Deliverable D4.3.1, NeP4B Project (2009)

13. Gennaro, C., Lenzi, R., Mandreoli, F., Martoglia, R., Mordacchini, M.: Design of procedures for building inter-peer semantic mapping. Deliverable D4.2.1, NeP4B Project (2009)

14. Gennaro, C., Mandreoli, F., Martoglia, R., Mordacchini, M., Orlando, S., Penzo, W., Sassatelli, S., Tiberio, P.: Toward an Effective and Efficient Query Processing in the NeP4B Project. In: Proc. of ItAIS (2008)

15. Gennaro, C., Mordacchini, M., Orlando, S., Rabitti, F.: MRoute: A Peer-to-Peer Routing Index for Similarity Search in Metric Spaces. In: Proc. of DBISP2P (2007)

16. Hernandez, M.A., Miller, R.J., Haas, L.M.: Clio: A semi-automatic tool for schema mapping. In: SIGMOD Conference, p. 607 (2001)

17. Lodi, S., Mandreoli, F., Martoglia, R., Penzo, W., Sassatelli, S.: Semantic Peer, Here are the Neighbors You Want! In: Proc. of EDBT (2008)

18. Loscio, B.F., Salgado, A.C., Vidal, V.M.P.: Using agents for generation and maintenance of mediators. J. Braz. Comp. Soc. 8(1), 32–42 (2002)

19. Mandreoli, F., Martoglia, R., Penzo, W., Sassatelli, S.: SRI: Exploiting Semantic Information for Effective Query Routing in a PDMS. In: Proc. of WIDM (2006)

20. Mandreoli, F., Martoglia, R., Penzo, W., Sassatelli, S.: Data-sharing P2P Networks with Semantic Approximation Capabilities. Accepted for Pubblication on IEEE Internet Computing (2009)

21. Mandreoli, F., Martoglia, R., Penzo, W., Sassatelli, S., Villani, G.: SRI@work: Efficient and Effective Routing Strategies in a PDMS. In: Benatallah, B., Casati, F., Georgakopoulos, D., Bartolini, C., Sadiq, W., Godart, C. (eds.) WISE 2007. LNCS, vol. 4831, pp. 285–297. Springer, Heidelberg (2007)

22. Melnik, S., Garcia-Molina, H., Rahm, E.: Similarity Flooding: A Versatile Graph Matching Algorithm and ist Application to Schema Matching. In: Proc. of the 18th ICDE (2002)

23. Noy, N.F.: A survey of ontology-based approaches. SIGMOD Record 33(4), 65–70 (2004)

24. Palmonari, M., Guerra, F., Turati, A., Maurino, A., Beneventano, D., Valle, E.D., Sala, A., Cerizza, D.: Toward a unified view of data and services. In: Proceedings of the 1st International International Workshop on Semantic Data and Service Integration, Vienna, Austria (2007)
25. Rahm, E., Bernstein, P.A.: A survey of approaches to automatic schema matching. VLDB J. 10(4), 334–350 (2001)
26. Sajja, P.S.: Multi-agent system for knowledge-based access to distributed databases. Interdisciplinary Journal of Information, Knowledge, and Management 3 (2008)
27. Tatarinov, I., Halevy, A.: Efficient Query Reformulation in Peer Data Management Systems. In: Proc. of ACM SIGMOD (2004)
28. Zhang, H., Croft, W.B., Levine, B.N., Lesser, V.R.: A multi-agent approach for peer-to-peer based information retrieval system. In: AAMAS, pp. 456–463. IEEE Computer Society (2004)

Agents and Peer-to-Peer Computing: Towards P2P-Based Resource Allocation in Competitive Environments

Yoni Peleg and Jeffrey S. Rosenschein

School of Engineering and Computer Science,
The Hebrew University,
Jerusalem, Israel
{jonip,jeff}@cs.huji.ac.il

Abstract. Peer-to-peer frameworks are known to be robust and scalable to large numbers of agents. Recent resource allocation studies have leveraged this by using peer-to-peer frameworks for the implementation of resource matching algorithms. In this paper, we present a matching protocol for multiagent resource allocation in a competitive peer-to-peer environment; this work marks the first solution to the resource matching problem in this type of environment. Our approach makes use of micro-payment techniques, along with concepts from random graph theory and game theory. We provide an analytical characterization of our protocol, and specify how an agent should choose optimal values for the protocol parameters.

1 Introduction

Resource allocation [1] is a fundamental problem in multiagent systems, allowing agents to share resources so as to complete their tasks. In this paper, we consider one important aspect of the problem, namely the *matching* problem. The goal is to match a supplier (an agent that can provide a resource) to a customer (an agent that needs the resource). We present a protocol that solves this problem in competitive environments; the protocol itself is based on a peer-to-peer (P2P) architecture, along with a central player.

P2P systems have become popular in recent years as a means of disseminating information in distributed environments. An important property of P2P systems is that control is distributed symmetrically among peers, increasing the systems' robustness and scalability.

Many practical P2P solutions are actually based on hybrid architectures: message distribution relies on a distributed peer architecture, while solutions for certain specific problems rely on some centralized entity (e.g., "BitTorrent Trackers" in BitTorrent, and "Rendezvous peers" in JXTA). In this paper we adopt this hybrid approach, and solve certain security problems in our P2P network using a central entity.

We assume that all agents in our system are self-interested, and thus concerned with maximizing their private utilities. An agent will not share its resources for

D. Beneventano et al. (Eds.): AP2PC 2008/2009, LNAI 6573, pp. 129–140, 2012.

free, and it will deviate from our protocol if by doing so it will increase its utility. The assumption of self-interested agents operating in the P2P environment is realistic for many scenarios, but introduces several challenges for incentivizing adherence in order to get a stable protocol [2]. This work marks the first solution to the resource matching problem in this type of environment.

We begin our discussion by providing an informal overview of the problem and our solution in Section 2. In Section 3, we explain our approach to the challenges alluded to above, using cryptographic techniques, random graph theory, and game theory. In Section 4, we give a formal description of the protocol, and in Section 5 we present an analysis of it. Section 6 discusses related work, and we conclude in Section 7.

2   An Overview of Our Approach

To help ensure that self-interested agents follow our protocol, we incorporate a payment mechanism into it. Each agent in the system has an account with some amount of virtual money. When a customer looks for a resource, it initiates an auction for that resource. Each possible supplier may send a bid to the customer; the customer then selects the best bid.

Our protocol makes use of Vickrey Auctions [3]. As in first price auctions, the supplier that offers the lowest bid wins; however, in Vickrey Auctions the customer pays the winner according to the offer of the second-lowest bid. It is well-known that in Vickrey Auctions, all bidders have a dominant strategy to bid their true private valuations. Additionally, Vickrey Auctions give suppliers an incentive to participate—if a supplier wins the auction, it benefits from the difference between its bid and the second-lowest bid.

To implement the auction, the customer sends agents *Auction Messages* informing them that an auction is taking place. The customer may not know all agents in the P2P network, and relies on its neighbors to keep forwarding the auction messages to *their* neighbors. We call each agent that needs to forward an auction message a *middle agent*; these middle agents will be paid for forwarding auction messages (this compensates middle agents for the effort they expend in transmitting those messages). Payments to middle agents are actually a critical part of the protocol, since each potential supplier has a natural incentive *not* to forward auction messages: the fewer participants in an auction, the higher its probability of winning. Paying for message forwarding is thus a necessity, to incentivize adherence to the protocol. This problem is discussed further in Section 3.4.

2.1   The Search Algorithm

We do not wish to restrict the definition of a resource, but want to allow it to be anything: CPU time, disk space, or even some task that an agent wants to outsource. Thus, we cannot use sophisticated *structured searches* [4] (like Distributed Hash Tables), but rather need to use *unstructured searches*.

Unstructured searches are usually based on flooding techniques or on random-walk techniques (see [5] for an excellent survey). Random-walk techniques are known to have lower message complexity than flooding techniques [6]. We, however, have chosen to use a flooding technique [7]; using this approach gives us a higher probability that more than one path will exist from the customer to a possible supplier. Thus, a potential supplier will not be able, on its own, to block many other possible suppliers. This subject is discussed further in Section 3.4.

Our search algorithm can be considered as an extension to Vanzin's work [8]; the following is a short overview of the algorithm:

1. The customer chooses auction parameters: TTL (Time To Live), l, and $Time$-Out and it pays for the auction accordingly.
2. The customer forwards auction messages to l of its neighbors (chosen uniformly at random among its neighbors) with the TTL and l parameters attached.
3. Each middle agent subtracts 1 from the message's TTL value, and forwards the message to l of its neighbors. When $TTL = 0$, agents no longer forward the message. If the agent is a possible supplier, it sends a bid to the customer.
4. The customer waits for $TimeOut$ seconds. It then either chooses the lowest bid, or starts a new auction.

2.2   Challenges to Overcome

The following list describes situations where a rational agent might deviate from the protocol:

- A middle agent gets paid for forwarding an auction message, and then does not forward the message. The customer cannot tell whether a middle agent has forwarded the auction message;
- A middle agent forwards the auction message, but the customer then denies that the auction ever existed, and refuses to pay for it;
- A middle agent falsely claims that another agent is searching for a resource, and charges that other agent for forwarding its auction message;
- A middle agent tries to get paid more than once;
- Using fake IDs—a middle agent may try to add itself more than once to the system, and then make money from forwarding the auction messages to itself;
- The customer claims that the value of the second-lowest bid was lower than it really was, paying the auction winner less.

2.3   Comparison with Existing Solutions

Our solution is a hybrid P2P protocol; to overcome the above difficulties, our solution uses a central trusted third party (Section 3.1). The number of messages that this third party entity receives depends only on the number of customers in the system. The number of messages in previous centralized solutions (like centralized match-makers, centralized internet directories, mechanism design algorithms, and "stable marriage problem" algorithms) also depends on the number of suppliers in the system, since each supplier needs to inform the central entity about the goods it can supply. Our solution is thus more scalable than those previous centralized solutions, despite our use of a central player in the protocol. In addition, our solution does not restrict the definition of a resource. Previous solutions (like centralized match-makers) had to make prior assumptions about the resources' definition.

3   Protocol Incentives

This section describes the incentives added to the protocol in order to overcome the difficulties listed above in Section 2.2. We make the following assumptions: agents are rational, are only aware of their immediate neighbors, and cannot fake identities nor form coalitions. The agents' utilities are determined by the amounts of money they have—each agent receives money for each task it completes, and receives $1 for each message it forwards. We also make a simplifying assumption that agents are not familiar with the private valuations of other agents in the system: an agent cannot estimate its probability of winning an auction based on its private bid.

3.1   The Central Bank

Our solution uses a central trusted third party called the bank, a secure entity that always follows the protocol. It handles the agents' accounts (that initially contain $0), and is in charge of money transfers. The bank also performs sporadic checks to help ensure that agents will not deviate from the protocol (details below).

3.2   Cryptographic Solutions

Giving incentives to agents to forward messages is a problem that has been studied extensively in recent years in the field of multi-hop cellular networks. In this paper, we follow a micro-payment solution that was presented by Jakobsson [9]. We begin by presenting a naive algorithm that solves the problem.

When an agent receives an auction message, it sends a message to the bank that includes a receipt (a cryptographic-hash signature of the message), and the ID of the agent from which it got the message (the previous agent in the search path). The bank pays $1 to the agent and $1 to the previous agent in the search path. In this way, each agent has an incentive to forward the message, since once the next agent gets the message the sending agent will also get paid (in its role as the previous agent in the search path).

The naive approach has a clear disadvantage: the bank is overloaded with messages. Jakobsson's solution to this problem is to use *Lottery Tickets*: each time an agent enters the system, it receives from the bank a private random integer s_i. Each time a customer starts an auction, it receives from the bank a random integer L which is the "lottery ticket". The bank signs L using its private

RSA key [10], so that each agent can verify the signature. When a middle agent gets an auction message, it can check with a known cryptographic-hash function H whether it won the lottery (for example, the agent wins the lottery if and only if $H(s_i, L) = 1$). An agent contacts the bank only if it won the lottery.

We can set the probability of winning to be small enough, so that the expected number of times the bank will be contacted in an auction will be 2. Once an agent wins the lottery, the bank gives it and the previous agent in the search path a very high payment, so in expectation the agent gets that same $1, as it got in the naive solution above. If the agent participates in many auctions, the average payment for forwarding an auction message will be close to the expectation.

Since we are using a cryptographic hash function, an agent cannot reveal another agent's secret number from previous auctions. Therefore, a middle agent cannot know in advance if the next agent will win the lottery, and thus it has an incentive to forward the message.

3.3 Solutions Based on the Bank

In the cryptographic solution from Section 3.2, the bank does not keep track of the entire message distribution process. Instead, the bank is prompted only when an agent wins the lottery. This gives rise to some additional challenges that our protocol must confront: agents may continue to forward the auction message when the TTL parameter is 0; they may send the auction message to more than l of their neighbors; they may lie about the identity of the previous agent in the search path. All these problems can be solved using cryptographic techniques; the bank needs to run sporadic checks to make sure that agents do not deviate in these ways (if the bank detects that an agent has deviated, it punishes that agent). We omit details due to lack of space—we refer the reader to [11] for further details.

3.4 Game Theory Solutions

A Two-Player Coordination Game. Consider the example network in Figure 1. The network contains four agents: $a, b, c,$ and d. a is a customer that starts an auction for a resource. $b, c,$ and d may supply the resource. Since a possible supplier will make a profit from winning an auction, b and c have a dilemma: if any of them forward the auction message, all three suppliers will participate in the auction; the probability of each of the agents to win decreases (and thus the expected profit from participating in the auction also decreases). If If neither of them do not forward the auction message, only b and c will participate in the auction, and their expected profit from participating in the auction will increase. b is worse off if c forwards the auction message while it does not—this way it will not get money for forwarding the auction message, and it will not increase its expected profit from participating in the auction. c has a symmetric situation. Thus we see that b and c are playing a coordination game: each of them can Cooperate (forward the auction message) or Defect (deviate from the protocol).

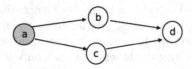

Fig. 1. A Sample Network

The Distribution of Private Valuations over Resources. To make the discussion above more concrete, we give a formal description of the agents' private valuation of resources. We assume that the agent's private valuation of a resource r is drawn i.i.d. from a distribution D_r. Thus, if there are m possible suppliers, each of them has probability $\frac{1}{m}$ of winning the auction. The winner is expected to offer the first-order statistics of the distribution D_r (given m participants); its expected profit will be the difference between the second and the first-order statistic.

To simplify our presentation, for the rest of the paper we take D_r to be the continuous uniform distribution on $[A_r, B_r]$. Nevertheless, all the calculations we present can be applied to any arbitrary distribution. We use the following known theorem [12]:

Theorem 1. *Let $X_1, X_2, \ldots, X_n$ be n random variables that were drawn from a continuous uniform distribution on the section $[A, B]$. Let Y_k be the k-th order statistics of $(X_i)_{i=1}^{n}$ (i.e., the k-th smallest value that was drawn). Then $E(Y_k) = A + (B - A)\frac{k}{n+1}$.*

Furthermore, throughout the rest of the paper we assume that $A_r = 0$. A different value of A_r simply means that a customer would need to pay at least A_r dollars in order to use the resource; it will not influence the expected profit of the suppliers, nor the customer's search strategy. Assuming that $A_r = 0$, both the expected bid of the winner and the expected profit of the winner are $\frac{B_r}{m+1}$.

Analysis of the above 2-Player Coordination Game using the continuous uniform distribution gives the game in Table 1 (below).

Table 1. The Sample Network Game Table

	C	D
C	(B/12)+1 (B/12)+1	B/12 (B/12)+1
D	(B/12)+1 B/12	B/6 B/6

If $B_r \leq 12$, then by Table 1 both agents have the dominant strategy of following the protocol. Unfortunately, usually we would expect the price of a resource to be much larger than the cost of forwarding a single message. If $B_r > 12$, we will get a coordination game where both CC and DD are Nash equilibria.[1] The DD strategy is Pareto optimal. Recall that we assume no coalitions, so agents b and c cannot coordinate with one another.

Boyer [14] has shown analytically that without prior conventions that help the agents coordinate, the system might converge to either a CC or DD equilibrium (even though CC is *not* Pareto optimal). Cooper [15] got the same results empirically. Furthermore, the following conventions might help the system converge to the CC equilibrium in practice:

- A rational agent might prefer a *Minimax* strategy that promises it the \$1 payment, rather than playing a strategy that in the worst case would leave it with nothing.
- An agent that is not a supplier has a dominant strategy to cooperate. This may provide a convention in favor of the CC equilibrium for unpopular resources.
- There may be multiple paths from the customer to the supplier (e.g., from a to d in Figure 1). In such a case, it is sufficient that the agents along one of the paths cooperate so as to turn cooperation into the best strategy for other agents.
- If no agents cooperate, the system will eventually crash. This can provide the agents a prior-convention to cooperate [16].

Multi-Player Coordination Games. In the network of Figure 1, we have a relatively simple coordination game with only two participants. Real networks are obviously far more complicated. As in the two-player game, multiple-player coordination games [17] may have more than one Nash equilibrium, and without further assumptions one cannot give a mathematical argument regarding which of the equilibria the system will converge to (even when one of the equilibria is Pareto optimal). We will show in Section 5.3 that in some cases it is possible to derive sufficient conditions for cooperation even without further assumptions.

If the agents to play a minimax strategy, stronger sufficient conditions can be deduced. Let T be a random number that represents the total number of agents that will accept the auction message if an agent cooperates. Let V be a random number that represents the total number of agents that will *surely* be blocked if the agent deviates (i.e., all the paths of length at most TTL to those V agents pass through the agent). According to our hypothesis, the agent will surely cooperate if: $B * \frac{2*V*T - V^2}{(T-V)^2 * T^2} \geq 1$. The values of T and V depend on the random graph model of the network. We show in Section 5.3 how these values can be approximated using "node coverage".

Why Don't We Use Payments Instead? Could we not simply pay more to middle agents for forwarding messages, such that cooperation becomes a

---

[1] For the rest of the paper we only consider ex-ante Nash equilibria (we make the simplifying assumption that agents have full knowledge of the network structure, and of other suppliers, a standard assumption, e.g., in papers on "byzantine and rational" network behavior [13]). Evaluating ex-post Nash equilibria is left for future research.

dominant strategy? Unfortunately, that approach increases the cost of each auction significantly, and reduces the probability of finding a resource. The details are omitted due to lack of space; a detailed explanation can be found in [11].

4   Our Protocol

We now introduce our detailed protocol (Algorithm 1, below) for carrying out an auction.

Algorithm 1. The protocol that is executed when a customer v_i holds an auction for a resource

1: The customer sets the auction parameters: $TimeOut$, l, and TTL. It connects to the bank and informs the bank that it wants to start an auction for a resource. The bank calculates the expected payment and charges the customer.
2: The bank generates a random number (the lottery ticket) L, signs it using its private key, and sends the signed message to the customer.
3: The customer sends the auction message (including the parameters and L) to l of its neighbors.
4: Each middle agent j that receives the auction message verifies the bank's signature on L; it checks if it won the lottery (if so, it informs the bank); it checks if it is a possible supplier (and submits a bid if it is). Eventually, it decreases the TTL value by 1 and forwards the message to l of its neighbors.
5: If the bank receives a winner announcement, it verifies that the agent indeed won, and it pays the agent and the previous agent in the search path. The bank does sporadic checks that the win is legitimate, and otherwise the bank punishes the previous agent in the search path.
6: The customer waits $TimeOut$ seconds, and then informs the bank of the best two bids. It uses the resource of the winner. The bank charges the customer and pays the winner.

4.1   Optimal Parameters for an Auction

The customer needs to choose three parameters for each auction: TTL, $TimeOut$, and l. Vanzin [8] describes how to choose the optimal value for the $TimeOut$ parameter. A rational customer always chooses l to be as large as possible,[2] since a larger l implies that each agent can block a smaller group of agents by itself. The optimal value of the TTL parameter depends on the level of cooperation among agents. Let us assume that all agents cooperate. We follow Wu's definition [6] of *node coverage* and let $N(j)$ be a random number that represents the number of agents at distance at most j from the customer. The optimal TTL is the value that minimizes the following expression: $|N(TTL) - \frac{\sqrt{2(B_r - A_r) * P_r - 1}}{P_r}|$.

---

[2] We assume that the degree of the vertices in the P2P network is bounded by a constant; otherwise, we would have broadcast capabilities.

The above expression holds if all agents follow the protocol. In Section 5.3 we show that this expression is correct in many cases even if the agents are simply rational. In Section 5.2 we give expressions for the node coverage ($N(j)$) of two popular random graphs.

4.2 Known Disadvantages

Our protocol does not demonstrate "fairness": if an agent is slow, it may not hear about/participate in an auction before the auction is over. Our protocol is also not budget-balanced. Since the environment is asynchronous, we cannot know in advance how many agents will participate in an auction (even if we have full knowledge of the network, and even if all agents cooperate). Thus, the customer might be overcharged for an auction. Furthermore, we cannot return the overcharged money back into the environment, since that would give agents an incentive to deviate from the protocol. More details can be found in [11].

5 Analysis of the Protocol

We here present a short analysis of the protocol. The analysis considers two graph models [18]: the *d-out* model, and the random geometric graph (RGG) model. We assume that each agent holds a resource with equal probability p. Due to lack of space, we omit proofs of theorems and most simulation results. Full descriptions of the simulations and the proofs of the theorems can be found in [11].

5.1 Graph Models

In the random d-out model, each vertex is connected to exactly d neighbors that are chosen uniformly. Duplicate edges and self-loops are not allowed. In the RGG model, the vertices' locations are distributed uniformly on an $L \times L$ board. There is an edge between two agents if and only if the distance between them is smaller than a threshold r.[3]

5.2 Node Coverage

The following two theorems approximate the node coverage in the d-out and RGG models:

Theorem 2. *Node coverage in the d-out model is (where $L_{d,n} = log_d(\sqrt{n})$):*
$E(X_j) \geq d^j$ *if* $0 \leq j \leq L_{d,n}$
$E(X_j) \geq \sqrt{n} * (d - \frac{2}{d})^{j-L_{d,n}}$ *if* $j \leq log_d(n) - 2$
$E(X_j) \geq \sqrt{n} * (\frac{d^2-2}{d})^{j-L_{d,n}}((d-2) * (1 - e^{-1}))$ *if* $j < 2L_{d,n}$
with high probability and $E(X_j) \leq d^j$, *where* $X_j = N(j) - N(j-1)$.

---

[3] We use the L_∞ norm in this presentation because it enables cleaner expressions.

Theorem 3. *Let $G(n, r, L)$ be an RGG where $L = 1$, $4r^2n = d$, $d \geq 30$. Let $j < \frac{L}{2r}$. Then with high probability: $\frac{n}{4} * (2 * j * (r - \frac{r}{\alpha}))^2 \leq N(j) \leq n * (2 * j * r)^2$.*

To evaluate our approximation, we compared it with simulation results. The simulation and analytic results were quite similar (9% average error on the RGG model, with standard deviation of 1%, 6.38% average error on the d-out model, with standard deviation of 0.01%). Our approximation is tighter than the approximation given by Wu [6].

5.3   Agent Cooperation

In the previous section, we demonstrated how to calculate the optimal *TTL* value for the case where all agents follow the protocol. A natural question that arises is, if we use that *TTL* value, will rational agents follow the protocol?

Theorem 4 gives a sufficient condition for cooperation without using assumptions about prior conventions. It relies on the fact that agents that cannot supply the resource have a dominant strategy to follow the protocol. Thus, agents cooperate if the resource is not popular.

Theorem 4. *A sufficient condition for cooperation in the d-out graph model is that:* $\frac{2}{d(d-1)^2} \leq \frac{p^2[d(1-p)]^{2TTL-2}}{B_r}$.

Unfortunately, our simulation results show that for popular resources, if we assume that there are no prior conventions then the optimal *TTL* for the auction is larger than the optimal *TTL* for a cooperative environment.

The next two theorems assume that agents have a prior convention to play minimax (Section 3.4).

Theorem 5. *In the d-out model, with high probability all agents will cooperate if:* $\frac{2}{d}\left(B_r + P_r^2\sqrt{\frac{2B}{P}}\right)exp\left(-\frac{1}{n}\sqrt{\frac{2B_r}{P_r}}\right) \leq 2B_r * P_r$.

Theorem 6. *In the RGG model, if $r \geq \sqrt{\frac{30L^2}{4n}}$ then all agents will follow the protocol.*

The idea behind Theorem 5 is that if the resource is expensive enough or if the resource is not popular, the customer will choose an auction with a large *TTL*. Thus, the number of possible suppliers that can be effectively blocked by a single agent is small, and the minimax strategy will cause the agents to cooperate. Clearly, if the resource is cheap, cooperation also becomes a dominant strategy. That leaves us with an (exponentially small) gap of intermediate prices, where an agent may deviate from the protocol. Simulations on the d-out model show that even for "problematic" intermediate prices, in about 95% of auctions all the agents in the system cooperate (recall that Theorem 5 gives only sufficient conditions for cooperation). From Theorem 6 we see that in the RGG model there is a "connectivity gap"; above it, agents will always follow the protocol. Unfortunately, the message complexity of our protocol in an RGG is much higher than in the d-out model.

6 Related Work

Chevaleyre et al. [1] is an excellent resource allocation survey; here, we briefly mention some related work on resource allocation matching. Much prior research used a central agent (e.g., [19]), which causes scalability problems. Mullender and Vitanyi [20] used a distributed matching process, and proved a $\sqrt{n}$ lower bound for the number of agents with which each matchmaker is familiar, assuming that matchmakers cannot pass information among themselves; thus, that work also has scalability problems when n is very large. Recent studies (e.g., Vanzin [8], Ogston and Vassiliadis [21]) have used a P2P matchmaking framework. Unlike our work, they assume a cooperative environment, and identical resources. The well-known Contract Net protocol [22] used auctions for matchmaking, and was later extended to non-cooperative environments. However, the Contract Net relied on broadcasts for carrying out auctions, which is very inefficient if a natural broadcast channel does not exist.

7 Conclusions

We have presented a protocol that addresses the resource allocation matching problem. The protocol is based on a P2P framework with a centralized bank; the central bank plays a role different in our protocol from its role in previous solutions, allowing our technique to be more scalable than those previous approaches.

The protocol is designed for non-cooperative environments—incentives are provided for the agents to follow the protocol, and we showed sufficient conditions that ensure that the incentives will indeed cause all agents to follow the protocol.

Three important topics are open for future work. First, simulation results show that our protocol withstands coalitions of constant size; a formal analysis of this remains open. Another interesting question is whether we can distribute the role of the central bank, doing away with the one centralized aspect of our solution (a similar approach was taken in [23]). Finally, dealing with "whitewashing" (detecting and punishing participants that use fake IDs) is one of the most important open problems in P2P research.

References

1. Chevaleyre, Y., Dunne, P., Endriss, U., Lang, J., Lemaitre, M., Maudet, N., Padget, J., Phelps, S., Rodriguez-Aguilar, J., Sousa, P.: Issues in multiagent resource allocation. Informatica 30 (2005)
2. Zlotkin, G., Rosenschein, J.S.: Mechanisms for automated negotiation in state oriented domains. Journal of Artificial Intelligence Research 5, 163–238 (1996)
3. Vickrey, W.: Counterspeculation, auctions, and competitive sealed tenders. The Journal of Finance 16, 8–37 (1961)
4. Risson, J., Moors, T.: Survey of research towards robust peer-to-peer networks: search methods. Computer Networks 50, 3485–3521 (2006)

 5. Li, X., Wu, J.: Searching techniques in peer-to-peer networks. In: Handbook of Theoretical and Algorithmic Aspects of Ad Hoc, Sensor, and Peer-to-Peer Networks, pp. 1–28 (2006)
 6. Wu, B., Kshemkalyani, A.D.: Analysis models for blind search in unstructured overlays. In: NCA 2006: Proceedings of the Fifth IEEE International Symposium on Network Computing and Applications, pp. 223–226. IEEE Computer Society, Washington, DC (2006)
 7. Kalogeraki, V., Gunopulos, D., Zeinalipour-Yazti, D.: A local search mechanism for peer-to-peer networks. In: CIKM 2002: Proceedings of the Eleventh International Conference on Information and Knowledge Management, pp. 300–307. ACM, New York (2002)
 8. Vanzin, M.M., Barber, K.S.: Decentralized partner finding in multiagent systems. Coordination of Large-Scale Multiagent Systems, 75–98 (2006)
 9. Jakobsson, M., Hubaux, J.-P., Buttyán, L.: A Micro-Payment Scheme Encouraging Collaboration in Multi-hop Cellular Networks. In: Wright, R.N. (ed.) FC 2003. LNCS, vol. 2742, pp. 15–33. Springer, Heidelberg (2003)
10. Rivest, R.L., Shamir, A., Adelman, L.M.: A method for obtaining digital signatures and public-key cryptosystems. Technical Report MIT/LCS/TM-82, MIT (1977)
11. Peleg, Y.: Towards P2P-based resource allocation in competitive environments. Master's thesis, School of Engineering and Computer Science, The Hebrew University of Jerusalem (2009)
12. Ahsanullah, M.: Order Statistics. Nova (2005)
13. Clement, A., Li, H., Napper, J., Martin, J.P., Alvisi, L., Dahlin, M.: Bar primer. In: IEEE International Conference on Dependable Systems and Networks With FTCS and DCC, DSN 2008, pp. 287–296 (2008)
14. Boyer, R., Orlean, A.: How do conventions evolve? Journal of Evolutionary Economics 2, 165–177 (1992)
15. Cooper, R., De Jong, D.V., Forsythe, R., Ross, T.W.: Forward induction in coordination games. Economics Letters 40, 167–172 (1992)
16. Feldman, M., Papadimitriou, C., Chuang, J., Stoica, I.: Free-riding and whitewashing in peer-to-peer systems. IEEE Journal on Selected Areas in Communications 24, 1010–1019 (2006)
17. Huyck, J.B.V., Battalio, R.C., Beil, R.O.: Tacit coordination games, strategic uncertainty, and coordination failure. The American Economic Review 80, 234–248 (1990)
18. Zegura, E., Calvert, K., Bhattacharjee, S.: How to model an internetwork. In: Proceedings of IEEE Fifteenth Annual Joint Conference of the IEEE Computer Societies. Networking the Next Generation, INFOCOM 1996, vol. 2, pp. 594–602 (1996)
19. Bertels, K., Panchanathan, N., Vassiliadis, S., Ebrahimi, B.P.: Centralized matchmaking for minimal agents. In: Proceedings of the Conference on Parallel and Distributed Computer Systems (ICPADS), p. 9 (2004)
20. Mullender, S.J., Vitanyi, P.M.B.: Distributed match-making. Algorithmica 3, 367–391 (1987)
21. Ogston, E., Vassiliadis, S.: Matchmaking among minimal agents without a facilitator. In: International Conference on Autonomous Agents, AAMAS (2001)
22. Smith, R.G.: The contract net protocol: high-level communication and control in a distributed problem solver. IEEE Transactions on Computers 12, 1104–1113 (1980)
23. Zhong, S., Chen, J., Yang, Y.R.: Sprite: a simple, cheat-proof, credit-based system for mobile ad-hoc networks. In: Twenty-Second Annual Joint Conference of the IEEE Computer and Communications Societies, INFOCOM 2003, vol. 3, pp. 1987–1997. IEEE (2003)

A Colored Petri Net Model
to Represent the Interactions between
a Set of Cooperative Agents

Toktam Ebadi, Maryam Purvis, and Martin K. Purvis

Department of Information Science, University of Otago,
11th Floor, Commerce Building, 60 Clyde Street,
Dunedin, New Zealand
{tebadi,tehrany,mpurvis}@infoscience.otago.ac.nz

Abstract. This paper describes an application of modelling multi agent systems in the context of multi-robot cooperation for performing tasks. It uses a layered approach based on Colored Petri Nets for modelling complex, concurrent conversations among agents in a multi-agent system. In this approach each agent employs the implementation of a Petri Net model that allows agents to follow a plan specifying their interactions. It also allows programmers to plan for the concurrent feature of the conversation and make sure that all possible states of the problem space are considered. Moreover, the system performance is examined under various agents strategies for finding teammates and performing the task.

1 Introduction

Climate change will cause more disasters to occur in the near future and thus rapid and effective response to disaster victims is very important. In disasters there may be some areas that are not safe for humans to operate. For instance some areas may be contaminated with chemicals or radioactive particles. In these situations using robots could be extremely helpful. Here we study such scenarios in which people are trapped in an unsafe area and a group of robots with different capabilities may be required to save the victims. This work employs CPN (Colored Petri Net) models for programming agents when cooperation of a team of robotic agents for completing a task is required. CPNs offer concurrent modelling at a high abstraction level which provides formal models with mathematical formalism. CPNs are well suited for simulating, analyzing and modelling distributed and concurrent systems [1]. CPNs can express a wide range of interactions in graphical representation and have well defined semantics. The theoretical aspects of Petri Nets allow precise modelling and analysis of system behaviour, while the graphical representation of Petri nets facilitates intuitive understanding of the proposed solution. In addition, the modular and hierarchical aspects of the Petri Net models can help in designing solutions for complex systems [2].

In the present work agents have different capabilities (at various levels) required for different tasks. The capabilities are designed in such a way that each

D. Beneventano et al. (Eds.): AP2PC 2008/2009, LNAI 6573, pp. 141–152, 2012.
© Springer-Verlag Berlin Heidelberg 2012

agent is expert only at one capability, so cooperation of a team of agents is required to complete a task. Tasks are heterogeneous and have various requirements which can be satisfied by capabilities of agents. In addition to capabilities, some agents (skilled agents) are assumed to be equipped with some devices which can locate the tasks and recognise the task requirements. Due to the presumed high cost of these devices, there may be a limited number of such agents equipped with these parts. All the other agents (helper agents) without any task discovery device can be recruited by skilled agents to perform the tasks. Skilled agents explore the environment in order to find tasks. When a skilled agent detects a task, it creates a CPN model and puts the task information as a token into its CPN model. The initiator sends requests to its neighbouring agents asking for help. When a helper agent receives a message from an initiator, it creates a CPN model for that interaction and puts the message as a token into its CPN model. The agents participating in an interaction coordinate their activities by passing message tokens. More details on the CPN model are provided in section 5.

The rest of the paper is organized as follows. Section 2 discusses related work. Section 3 describes the agent platform and conversation handling module used in this work. Section 4 describes how the agents and the environment are modelled. Section 5 details the CPN models for representing the conversation protocol. Section 6 describes the different strategies that agents may employ, and experimental results are discussed in section 7. Section 8 concludes and outlines future work.

2   Related Work

Celaya et al. [4] performed preliminary research on methodologies for modeling, analysis and design of multi-agent systems. They used Petri nets as a modeling tool to assess the structural properties of the multi-agent systems. Their methodology consists of defining a simple multi-agent system based on the abstract architecture for intelligent agents. De Weyns et al. [5] proposed a Colored Petri Net for regional synchronization. With regional synchronization agents synchronize their actions with each other locally. This results in independent groups of synchronized agents. Their system is based on a two-phase commit protocol combined with a logical clock. They tested their model for only two agents and verified the correctness of their approach. Costelha et al. [6] introduced Petri net models to achieve cooperation between robots. They focused on plan analysis corresponding to checking if the resource consumption is stable and plans have no deadlocks. They also analyzed the stochastic performance of their system considering the plan success probability. Bonnet-Torres et al. [7] presented a general framework for representing a team plan based on Petri Nets. In their approach agents are organized in a team hierarchy, and a plan is represented by a hierarchical Petri Net whose places are agents activities. They used a projector operator that allows individual agents to derive plans from a team plan so agents know which agent to interact with for each activity. Coordination of the distributed team is achieved by a conjunction of individual agents plans.

The present work shows the usability of CPNs in cooperative scenarios where agents do not have the complete information about their environment. Each agent participating in a task only performs some part of a task, and coordination between teammates is achieved by passing message tokens between team members.

3 Agent Framework

3.1 Opal Agent and Conversation Manager

This work employs Opal agent platform [8] to support multi-robot cooperation. Opal is a FIPA-compliant agent platform. At the lowest level it contains micro-agents, which are non-FIPA Java objects which have agent-like properties and may run in their own thread. A typical Opal agent could contain numerous micro-agents to perform tasks such as dispatch message, manage conversation and execute planning. Opal has a module called Conversation Manager (CM). The CM uses CPN as the modelling language and is useful in handling agent conversations. Figure 1 shows the high level view of the Opal system. In Opal every agent has its own CM to manage its conversations. Each CM is capable of handling multiple conversations for a single agent. Each agent participating in a conversation has a role. The role information allows the CM to find an appropriate Petri Net model for handling that conversation. For creating a new

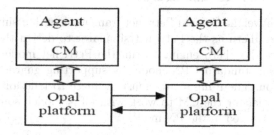

Fig. 1. The interaction between Opal agents and Opal platform

conversation, the initiating agent must know who is participating in the conversation and the role of each participating agent. When a message is sent from the initiator to a helper, if there is already such conversation (a conversation with that id) then it finds the CPN model of that conversation and handles the message, but if not, it creates a new conversation with that conversation id and handles the message. Figure 2 shows the interaction between different parts of the system for a simple request and response upon finding a task. After finding a task, the CM creates a local instance of conversation. It also creates a CPN model and puts the token (task and possible teammates information) into its CPN model. Then a request message is sent to available neighboring agents asking for help. The helper agent receives the request and passes it to its CM. The CM puts the message into the corresponding CPN model which processes the message and produces a response. The response is passed to CM which passes it to the agent. Then the agent sends the response to the requester. The requester then passes the message to CM and CM puts the message into the corresponding CPN model.

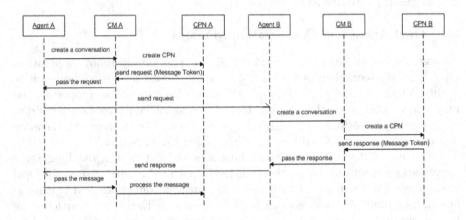

Fig. 2. The interaction between various parts of the system

3.2   Colored Petri Net and JFern

JFern [9] is a lightweight Colored Petri net framework with a simulator, written in Java. We used JFern as the Petri net simulator to design the CPN models. The CM requires the JFern engine to run the Petri net model of each agent. JFern extends the standard CPN model by supporting guards for each input arc of a transition. These input arcs must evaluate to true for a transition to be enabled. In order for the CM to work with CPN model, some special CPN places should be created in the PN model.

- *start*, *in* and *out*: For the initiator of a conversation.
- *in* and *out*: For helper agents in a conversation.

The *start* place: is only required for initiating the conversation (putting the token which includes the necessary information for the conversation like conversation id, the name of the interaction protocol).

The *in* place: all incoming messages to the agent are handled by the CM and relevant information associated with a message will be encapsulated in a token and inserted directly into this place.

The *out* place: Every token that reaches the output place will have information that contains sent as an agent message to the receiving agent. The receiving agent will take the received message and insert the relevant information into its *in* place of its appropriate CPN.

4   Environment and Agent Model

We simulated a physical environment divided into several spatial regions. A RFID tag is assumed to be deployed in each region and holds some information with respect to the geographical coordinates of the region. Task information is also stored in RFID tags which are distributed in some regions of the environment. The agents are equipped with limited range RFID readers that allow agents to position themselves in the environment by reading the coordinate information from environment tags. A few agents are equipped with longer range RFID readers in addition to the limited range readers which allow the agents to find tasks in their regions. Here agents deploy the FIPA [3] protocols for communication. Moreover, the environment has a monitoring agent which contains criteria and policies for rewarding agents.

4.1   Agent's Capabilities

Agents are assumed to have different capabilities that are useful in satisfying different task requirements. The capabilities of each agent are fixed and do not change over time. In this work each agent has two capabilities but is expert at one of them so cooperation of a team of agents is required to perform a task. The capability values, representing the quality level of the expertise, may range from 0 to 1.

4.2   Tasks

Tasks are distributed in the environment and have different requirements that should be satisfied by the different capabilities of the agents. A task is represented as a tuple:

$$< r, t, w >$$

r is the the set of requirements. The requirements range is set here to range between 0 and 1. t is the time constraint of the task. w is the basic reward that a team receives by performing the task. The reward is distributed equally to the participating agents if they can perform the task before time expires.

4.3   Agents Reward

The agents participating in performing a task receive a reward which is proportional to the total completed part of the task. All the agents participating in performing a task receive the same reward. For each agent the reward is calculated based on the following equation:

$$R = \sum_{i=1}^{n} \frac{\sum_{j=1}^{m} (A_j)_{cap(i)}}{r_i} \times \frac{w}{n}$$

n is the number of task requirements. m is the number of participating agents. r_i is the $i^{th} - requirement$ of the task. $(A_j)_{cap(i)}$ is the capability of the agent for $i^{th} - requirement$ and w is the basic task reward.

4.4   Agent Roles

- Initiator: is a skilled agent who is capable of detecting tasks. If an agent detects a task then it may start a new conversation to find teammates.
- Helper: An agent who has been asked for help by a skilled agent plays a helper role.

5   Modelling Agents Roles

In this work two models are designed based on the roles that agents could play in a conversation. Figures 3 and 5 show the CPN models for the initiator and helper role, respectively. In these models an environmental system time is used to accommodate the time delay associated with agents responses in a distributed multi-agent environment. This is to make sure that agents have a timeout mechanism and do not wait indefinitely for responses from other agents when they are not available.

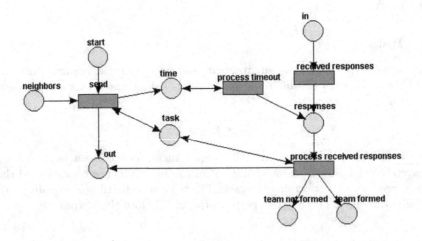

Fig. 3. The Petri Net model for the initiator role

Figure 3 has three different phases. In the first phase the agent sends requests to its neighbors and asks whether they could participate in performing the task. In the second phase the agent tries to form a team based on positive responses that it receives from the requested agents. In the third phase, the agent sends a move message to its selected teammates and a reject message to other agents who had responded positively but have not been selected by the initiator.

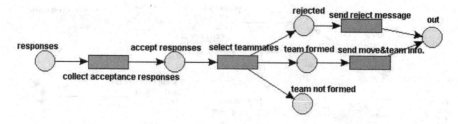

Fig. 4. Hierarchical view of the initiator PN for the *process received responses* transition

Phase 1: When an agent finds a task, it creates a token and puts it into the start place. The token has the task information (requirements, time constraint, and reward) and the name of the interaction protocol for the conversation. The names of the helper agents in the neighborhood are put into neighbors place. Then the agent sends help requests to its neighbors. After sending the requests, the sent time is put into the *time* place and then the agent waits until the waiting time elapses. Phase 2: After the waiting time elapses, the agent begins processing all the responses that it has received from other agents and selects its teammates. The guard on the arc that connects the *in* place to the *receive responses* transition filters the received messages and only allows messages with the accept or reject performative to be passed to the *process received responses* transition. Figure 4 shows a hierarchical view of the initiator Petri Net for the *process received responses* transition. The transition *collect acceptance responses* collects all the positive responses and the transition *select teammates* processes the positive responses. Phase 3: If the agent could find helper agents with the required capabilities, then a move message is sent to the selected teammates that directs the agents to move. This message also contains the details of the team. The agent also sends a reject message to all the agents who have responded positively but have not been selected as teammates, and informs them that they are not selected. If the agent cannot find agents with the required capabilities, then it drops its currents task and starts searching for new tasks.

Figure 5 shows the CPN model of the helper role. A helper agent receives requests from various initiators in its neighborhood (transition *receive request*). If the agent is involved in performing another task, then it sends a reject message to the requester agent (transition *send reject*). However, if the helper is available, then it may want to wait for a certain length of time to receive several requests and then select the best offer. The CPN model of the helper accommodates the waiting time by including the *process timeout* transition. After receiving a request, the helper agent puts the current time as a token into the *time* place. The *process timeout* transition compares the time that the first request was received with the current time. If the difference is more than the waiting time for helper agents, then it passes all the received requests to the *process request* transition otherwise, it puts the time token back to the *time* place. When waiting

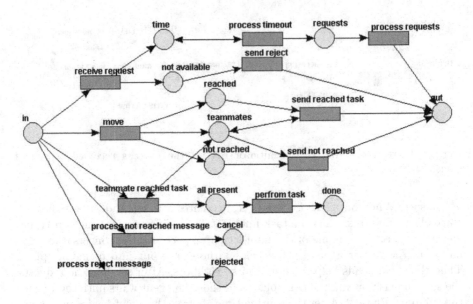

Fig. 5. The Petri Net model for the helper role

time has elapsed, the *process request* transition processes all the requests and selects the best offer and sends a positive response to the initiator and changes its status to unavailable.

A helper agent with a positive response to a request may be rejected by the initiator of the conversation if better-suited helpers are available. In this case the rejected agent changes its status to available and can participate in other tasks (transition *process reject message*). When a helper agent receives a move message from an initiator, it starts moving toward the task. The move message also contains the name of the teammates. After reaching the task location, it sends a message to its teammates informing them of its current location. When all the teammates are present at the task location, then the agents start performing the task. For performing a task, each agent has to spend some time at the task which is proportional to the part of the task that is to be completed by the agent. If the agent does not reach the task location after a certain period of time, then it sends a message to its teammates informing them about the issue (transition *send not reached*). In this situation all the team members cancel their current contract (transition *process not reached message*).

6   Strategies

Various strategies are designed for selecting teammates and tasks in the framework. These strategies allow measuring the performance of the system in scenarios when time is critical and agents must perform their tasks within a specified time.

Impatient: agents that employ this strategy do not wait to receive responses from all the requested agents, but select the first agents that respond to their requests as their teammates.

Nearest Available Strategy: An agent that employs this strategy selects an agent that lies at the least distance to the task and can perform some parts of a task. Agents with this strategy receive partial rewards proportional to the completed part of the task.

Best Available Strategy: Agents that employ this strategy gain partial rewards by partially completing tasks. These agents select the helper agents that provide a higher quality for task requirements. The quality refers to the agents capabilities with respect to the task requirement and is measured based on the following equation: $Q_A = \sum_{i=1}^{n} r_i \times A_{cap(i)}$ In this equation, n is the number of task requirement, r_i is the ith requirement of the task and $A_{cap(i)}$ is the capability of agent A that corresponds to the ith requirement of the task.

Best Possible Strategy: An agent that employs this strategy only selects another agent as its teammate if the two agents as a team can complete the task.

Delegation Strategy: Skilled agents with delegation strategy do not participate in performing tasks if they could find other agents to delegate their tasks to them. Skilled agents who do not employ this strategy include themselves as part of a team for performing tasks. By means of delegation, the skilled agent delegates the actual processing of the task to helper agents. This enables the agent to attempt to locate another task and coordinate a set of teammates who can complete the task.

7   Experiments

7.1   Experimental Setup

The experimental agent framework was tested by deploying Opal agents on a simulation grid-type environment. Note that while the developed framework was examined here by performing computer simulations of agent activity, the framework is ultimately intended for deployment on real, physical robots. Our multi-threaded simulation environment comes close to reproducing the concurrency conditions of real distributed multi-agent robotic systems. The framework allows agents to run multiple conversations over various tasks concurrently. The simulation environment is a grid of 100 by 100 cells in which each cell refers to one square of the grid. There are 64 robots with different capabilities. Out of 64 robots only 16 of them are able to detect the tasks. There are 150 tasks with different requirements placed randomly in the environment. Task requirements and agents capabilities are chosen randomly. The reward for each task is 7. The visibility range of all the agents is fixed to 10 cells. This allows agents to communicate with reasonable number of agents in their neighborhood at each point of time. The maximum waiting time was set to 60000 milliseconds. All times in this system are in milliseconds. In all the experiments there is some time associated with moving and performing the tasks. The moving time is a function of the distance between the agents and task positions, and the performance time is a function of the proportion of the task that has to be completed by the agent.

7.2   The Effect of Agents Task Selection Strategy on AgentS Reward

The aim of the first experiment is to show which strategy is suitable under certain conditions. In this experiment there were four groups of agents in which each group employed one strategy. Four different runs of simulation were performed under various time constraints. The total reward achieved by each group was measured under the time constraints of 500, 1000, 2000 and 3000 milliseconds.

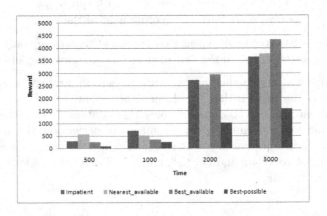

Fig. 6. The effect of task selection strategy on agents reward

Figure 6 shows when time was very tight (500) all groups performed somewhat impatiently due to lack of enough time. Therefore, agents with nearest-available strategy who selected the closest available teammate performed better than other groups. This is due to the fact that these agents have enough time to move toward their tasks and perform them. When time was a bit more relaxed (1000), then impatient strategy outperformed other strategies. When time was relatively relaxed (2000 and 3000), best-available strategy outperformed the other strategies. This is the result of selecting high-quality teammates. The agents with best-possible strategy performed worse under various time constraints. This is the effect of perfectionist attitudes of these agents. This approach is useful when there is more incentive in completing a job. For example, if there is a container full of poisonous and explosive chemical near to a building which is in fire and there are people trapped inside the building, then partially removing the explosive material is not enough.

7.3   The Effect of Delegating Strategy

In this experiment the effect of agents delegation strategy on performance time was studied. In this experiment agents with best-possible strategy are employed. Two different runs of simulation were performed. In one experiment, skilled agents were allowed to delegate and in the next experiment skilled agents had to stay committed to their current tasks (perform tasks). Figure 7 shows the effect

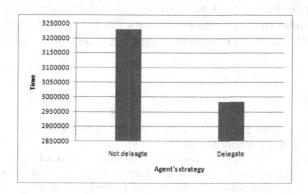

Fig. 7. The effect of agents delegation strategy on performance time

of agents delegation strategy on total time. By using the delegation strategy the total performance time decreased. This is due to the fact that skilled agents do not waste their time performing tasks that another helper agent might be capable of performing and instead spend their time on detecting other tasks and organizing teams to perform more tasks.

8   Conclusion

This paper introduced a general lightweight framework for enhancing cooperation among agents. The framework employs CPNs to model and execute concurrent activities of the agents. The agent robots communicate by employing the standard FIPA protocols. Employing the Conversation Manager module enabled us to deal with multi-threaded complexities associated with multiple concurrent conversations for a single agent. The agents obtain a CPN model based on their role in each conversation and start executing their CPN model. The coordination between agents is achieved by passing message tokens between CPN models of agents. In addition, the effect of various agents strategies on system performance was studied. The experiments showed that when time was tight and agents were allowed to perform the tasks partially, the nearest available strategy was suitable. When time demands were relatively tight, the impatient strategy performed better than other strategies. However, when time demands were more relaxed then the best available strategy was more suitable. The best possible strategy performed worse under various time constraints, and this was due to the initiator not being able to find enough agents with the required capabilities. Therefore in most cases theses agents are not successful in forming a team. Despite the poorer performance of the best possible strategy agents, there could be situations where partially performing a task is not possible or suitable, and thus the best possible strategy is appropriate. The second experiment showed the effect of delegation strategy in scenarios when agents are required to complete the task. The results showed that delegating strategy, under the given configuration, had improved the performance. Future work will involve explorations concerning how agents can optimally alter their strategies in dynamic environments. In addition, we will examine how the agent reputation in completing tasks can be used in teammate selection.

References

1. Jensen, K.: Coloured Petri Nets: Basic Concepts Analysis Methods and Practical Use, vol. 1. Springer, Berlin (1992)
2. Nowostawski, M., Purvis, M., Cranefield, S.: A layered approach for modelling agent conversations. In: Proceedings of the 2nd International Workshop on Infrastructure for Agents, MAS, and Scalable MAS, 5th International Conference on Autonomous Agents, Montreal, pp. 163–170 (2001)
3. FIPA, The foundation for Intelligent Physical Agents (2002),
   http://www.fipa.org/repository/index.html
4. Celaya, J.R., Desrochers, A.A., Graves, R.J.: Modeling and analysis of multi-agent systems using petri nets. In: The International Conference on Systems, Man and Cybernetics, Montreal, Que., pp. 1439–1444 (2007)
5. Weyns, D., Holvoet, T.: A Colored Petri Net for Regional Synchronization in Situated Multi-Agent Systems. In: the Proeedings of First International Workshop on Petri Nets and Coordination, Bologna, Italy, pp. 65–86 (2004)
6. Costelha, H., Lima, P.: Modelling, analysis and execution of multi-robot tasks using petri nets. In: The Proceedings of the 7th International Joint Conference on Autonomous Agents and Multiagent Systems, International Foundation for Autonomous Agents and Multiagent Systems, Richland, SC, pp. 1187–1190 (2008)
7. Bonnet-Torres, O., Tessier, C.: From team plan to individual plans: a petri net-based approach. In: The Proceedings of the Fourth International Conference on Autonomous Agents and Multiagent Systems, pp. 797–804. ACM, New York (2005)
8. Purvis, M., Nowostawski, M., Cranefield, S.: A multi-level approach and infrastructure for agent-oriented software development. In: The First International Conference on Autonomous agents and Multi Agent Systems, pp. 88–89. ACM Press, Bologna (2002)
9. Nowostawski, M.: JFern- Java-based Petri Net framework (2000)

Author Index

Amamiya, Makoto   83
Amamiya, Satoshi   83

Bergamaschi, Sonia   115
Botelho, Luís Miguel   71
Bourdon, François   47
Brazier, Frances   95

Cabri, Giacomo   104

Ebadi, Toktam   141
Eertink, Henk   59

Guerra, Francesco   115

Kafalı, Özgür   35
Kimura, Kousaku   83

Lenzini, Gabriele   59
Lopes, António Luís   71

Manavalan, Priyadarshini   13
Mandreoli, Federica   115

Mari, Marco   24
Mine, Tsunenori   83

Ogston, Elth   95

Peleg, Yoni   129
Poggi, Agostino   24
Pommier, Hugo   47
Purvis, Martin K.   1, 141
Purvis, Maryam   1, 141

Rosenschein, Jeffrey S.   129

Sahli, Nabil   59
Savarimuthu, Sharmila   1
Singh, Munindar P.   13

Tomaiuolo, Michele   24
Turci, Paola   24

Vincini, Maurizio   115

Warnier, Martijn   95

Yolum, Pınar   35